A Royal Tragedy

A Royal Tragedy

BEING THE STORY OF THE ASSASSINATION OF KING ALEXANDER AND QUEEN DRAGA OF SERVIA

Chedomille Mijatovich

Formerly Servian Minister at the Court of St. James's

With an introduction by John Van der Kiste

A & F Reprints

First published by Eveleigh Nash, London, 1906, and Dodd, Mead & Co, New York, 1907
First published by A & F 2020

Introduction copyright 2020 © John Van der Kiste

A & F Publications
South Brent, Devon, England TQ10 9AS

Typeset 11pt Charter

ISBN: 9798600617162

Cover: (front) King Alexandra, Queen Draga, and the Royal Palace, Belgrade; (back) Chedomillle Mijatovich

Printed by KDP

CONTENTS

Introduction   2
Preface   5
Illustrations   9

I. A strange prophecy   11
II. The birth of King Alexander   16
III. Sasha's childhood   22
IV. The silent boy king   29
V. How the silent Sasha became "Alexander the Great"   33
VI. King Alexander's second *coup d'état*   39
VII. Russia and Servia   44
VIII. Russia's rule in the ruin of Alexander   52
IX. Madame Draga Mashin   59
X. The regime of "work and order"   66
XI. Attempt on the life of King Milan   76
XII. On the eve of the fatal deed   89
XIII. Alexander's marriage with Draga Mashin   96
XIV. King Alexander and the Servian army   108
XV. The last interview with Queen Draga   112
XVI. The conspiracy   121
XVII. The assassination   128
Appendix   147

INTRODUCTION

Several crowned heads or their heirs met violent deaths during the first two decades of the twentieth century. The roll call included King Umberto II of Italy in 1900, King Carlos of Portugal and his elder son, Crown Prince Luis Filipe in 1908, King George I of Greece in 1913, Archduke Francis Ferdinand, heir to the Austro-Hungarian empire, and his morganatic wife Sophie in 1914, and the massacre of Nicholas II, former Tsar of Russia, and his family in 1918.

Yet with the exception of the last, the most brutal was undoubtedly the conspiracy in 1903 that resulted in the elimination of King Alexander and Queen Draga of Serbia (or Servia, as it was then known and is thus referred to throughout in this book), plus several members of their family and army officers loyal to them, in their palace at Belgrade. The King and Queen had been heartily disliked by their own countrymen, and once the news of their deaths became common knowledge it seems that they were little mourned. An editorial in *The Times* of London that same week wrote that 'never in modern Europe has a Palace Revolution taken place in a manner so sudden, so thorough-going, and so relentless'. It also noted that the hapless young King had 'been luckless from his birth … the son of a blackguardly father and of a highly excitable mother … from the beginning [he] was never given a chance'.

A glance through the paper's columns over the subsequent few days suggests that he and his Queen were hardly missed. 'The murder of the King and Queen and the suppression of the former Cabinet are stated to have been received in Belgrade and throughout the country with the utmost tranquillity. The crowds which filled the streets warmly acclaimed the new Ministers as they drove to the Ministry of the Interior.' Moreover, their bodies 'were subjected to shocking indignities' when the public were admitted to view them as they lay in state, while 'their burial was 'carried out practically in secret, and with indecent haste'. At the funeral ceremony only four priests were present, and most of the senior clergy were conspicuous by their absence. After a few days one particular correspondent was moved to write to the editor, deploring that it was 'both cruel and sad to see that hardly anywhere in the Continental Powers is to be found a word of sympathy for the slain Monarch and his Consort.'

Yet not surprisingly their fate aroused deep revulsion in those who had known them, and particularly among some of their fellow European sovereigns. In Germany, Emperor William II never ceased to regard the Serbs as regicides and their kingdom beneath contempt, while in England King Edward VII, who insisted that he belonged to 'a trade union, a guild of kings', declared that he could not overlook the barbarous murder of a fellow member of his profession. He would not allow Britain's diplomatic relations with Servia to be resumed until all the officers involved had been retired from the army three years later.

Chedomille Mijatovich, whose biography was published in 1906, was a distinguished Servian government minister, diplomat and author. Born in 1842, he served several terms as Minister of Finance and of Foreign Affairs in his own country, and – appropriately as a lifelong Anglophile - as Servian Minister in London. It was during what turned out to be his last term of office at the latter that the *coup* which he described in his book took place, and he was so horrified at the events that had taken place in his own country that he resigned his position and spent the rest of his life in London. It was rumoured, though apparently without foundation, that he was involved in a movement to try and make Edward VII's only surviving brother Arthur, Duke of Connaught, King of Servia. Despite his revulsion to the *coup*, in 1911 he met King Peter, Alexander's successor, in Paris, and as a result he became fully reconciled with the new regime. The author of several books, including history and fiction, and contributor of articles to *Encyclopedia Britannica* (including, appropriately, one on King Alexander), he died in 1932.

His book is an admirably sympathetic account of what he called, with understandable exaggeration, 'the greatest tragedy of the last hundred years', and the characters most closely involved. King Alexander, the product of an unsatisfactory and harsh upbringing, was thoroughly ill-suited to wear the crown of one of the most volatile territories in Europe, a land that in the memorable phrase of Archduke Francis Ferdinand, the would-be Emperor of Austria mentioned above, was known as home to 'murderers, rascals and a few plum trees'. Its monarchs were singularly ill-starred. King Milan, Alexander's father and predecessor, had been elevated to the throne in 1882 when the Principality of Servia became a kingdom. He had been Sovereign Prince since 1868 when his own predecessor, his cousin and legal guardian Michael, was assassinated (*see Chapter 1, p.12 below*). King Peter, who replaced Alexander on the throne when the Obrenovic dynasty was replaced by that of Karageorgevic, was fortunate enough to retain the crown until his death from natural causes in 1921 at the age of seventy-seven, but his son, another Alexander, the first King of Yugoslavia, also met his death at the hands of an assassin while on a state visit to France in 1934. His son Peter, who ascended the throne as a boy of eleven, was deposed in 1945 after the end of the Second World War when his kingdom became a republic. He settled in the United States, where he died in 1970, aged forty-seven, after a life of exile marked by depression and alcoholism.

Ex-King Milan settled in Vienna and died in 1901, aged forty-six, from pneumonia. His body was returned to Servia and he was buried at the Krusedol Monastery, Vojvodina. The *coup* of 1903 left his widow Nathalie the sole survivor of the Obrenovic dynasty. She donated her inheritance to the University of Belgrade, and to various Serbian churches and monasteries, and subsequently became a member of the Roman Catholic Church and a nun. For the rest of her life she continued to live in France, where she had spent most of the previous few years. She died there in 1941, aged eighty-one, and was buried at Lardy Cemetery, Seine et Oise.

The hapless young King Alexander, only child of two hopelessly mismatched parents, 'more sinned against than sinning', a boy who ascended the throne in his thirteenth year and 'looked as if he had been made of cold marble and not flesh and blood,' never had the potential to be another 'Alexander the Great'. Yet, although in places it might read more like a novel than a work of historical biography, Mijatovich's concise account remains a vivid, invaluable and for the most part even-handed account of a horrific chapter in the saga of European monarchy.

JOHN VAN DER KISTE

PREFACE

The murderers of King Alexander and Queen Draga, who on that gruesome dawn of the 11th June 1903 made themselves masters of Belgrade, and consequently of Servia, have taken care that many of the details of their terrible deed should not be made public. But those few details which could not be hidden were of such a revolting and horrible nature that the whole civilised world stood aghast; indeed, the conscience of the civilised nations has not yet recovered from the shock that it then received.

But the assassination of King Alexander and Queen Draga was more terrible, and the drama of King Alexander's destiny more tragical, than is generally known. It has seemed to me, in the interests of history and justice, that the world should learn the whole truth.

In presenting an historical sketch of the last years and sad end of the Obrenovich Dynasty I have no political object in view. An inscrutable Providence has enacted on the volcanic platform of a small Balkan State a tragedy, of which the extraordinary sadness must always arouse in the hearts of noble and generous men and women the deepest pity and sympathy. I intend to describe that tragedy. I wish impartially to relate all that can be justly and truthfully said for and against King Alexander and Queen Draga, that can explain that horrible deed, and all that can be said in justification —— or at least in extenuation —— of that crime. My desire is to tell the whole truth, and by truth to move my readers to pity the victims as well as the principal actors of this, the greatest tragedy of the last hundred years.

Before proceeding with the history of the last days of the dynasty Obrenovich I will introduce here the

DRAMATIS PERSONÆ.

KING ALEXANDER OF SERVIA. —— A young man in his twenty-seventh year, intelligent, patriotic in his own way, self-willed, with exaggerated ideas of his Kingship, somewhat blind towards the light of morality. Born under exciting circumstances, in the critical years of tender childhood he saw his parents hate each other and create a world scandal by fighting over the possession of his person, all the time professing love for him, but practically killing his love for them. In his thirteenth year he was made King of one of the most difficult countries in the world, abandoned by both his parents, delivered into the hands of cynical men, without proper moral education, taught to distrust everyone, or rather to hate everyone. Later he fell in love with and came under the influence of a handsome widow, some nine years older than himself, made her his Queen in the face of every opposition, and remained faithful to her to his death. This, the only love his heart deeply felt, gave the pretext to the old and permanent enemies of his dynasty to organise a conspiracy and to assassinate him.

QUEEN DRAGA OF SERVIA. —— A fascinating widow of a small Servian official. By her loveliness, beauty, and talents backed by descent from Nikola Lunyevitza, an intimate friend of the founder of the dynasty Obrenovich she moved the pity of Queen Nathalie to complete her education and to take her as one of her Court ladies (*Dame d'honneur*). At the villa of the Queen in Biarritz she became the object of King Alexander's love proposals, which she resisted for some time, but ultimately became his mistress, and, having obtained an absolute control over his will, made him marry her and make her his Queen. She loved him with an entire devotion, and hoped by good deeds to reconcile the people to her.

KING MILAN. —— Father of King Alexander, who voluntarily abdicated in favour of his son (1889), whom he loved and adored; he worked to obtain the hand of a German Princess for him, and had every prospect of succeeding, when his son unexpectedly married the widow Draga Mashin, closed the frontier of Servia against him, and behaved towards him with cruelty. King Milan shortly afterwards died of a broken heart in Vienna.

QUEEN NATHALIE. —— Mother of King Alexander, a beautiful, intelligent, self-willed and imperious woman, with a strange mixture of the Roumanian, Russian, Levantine blood in her veins, from the middle class of the Bessarabian nobility raised by King Milan to the station of a Queen, for which station she lacked proper qualities. She made, not without provocation, her husband's and her own life bitter and unhappy, and finished by hating everyone and everything she once loved: her husband, her son, Russia, Servia, the very Church in which she had been born. To paralyse King Milan's influence with his son she allowed her Court lady, Draga Mashin, to flirt with the young King; but, once awakened to the real facts, tried bravely to save him from his mistress when, unfortunately, it was too late.

RUSSIA. —— The great Orthodox and Slavonic Power exercised an overwhelming influence over the simple and naive Slavonic and Orthodox people of Servia, hating with implacable hatred King Milan for his refusal to continue to be a tool in her hands, and for his seeking for his own and his country's interests protection with Austria. To separate King Alexander from his father, and to close the doors of Servia for ever to the latter, Russia facilitated (if not invented) the programme of the marriage of King Alexander with the widow Draga Mashin, and helped very materially its execution.

PARTISANS OF THE DYNASTY KARAGEORGEVICH spread and deepened the dissatisfaction with Alexander, the childless and only representative of the dynasty Obrenovich, and organised conspiracies for his overthrow and for placing the Pretender, Prince Peter Karageorgevich, on the throne of Servia.

A GROUP OF SERVIAN OFFICERS —— some as partisans of Karageorgevich, others as single-minded patriots, others again from sordid motives —— decided to assassinate King Alexander and the more important of his Ministers and courtiers, as well as Queen Draga and her two brothers. At the head of the conspiracy was the brother-in-law of Draga, Colonel Alexander Mashin.

THE FINAL SCENE. —— Darkness at the Palace.

Shortly before the dawn of the 11th June 1903, murderers search after the hiding King and Queen; merciless assassination and most cruel mutilation of their bodies, ultimately thrown from a window of the first floor of the Palace, naked and with horrible wounds, down into the front garden in the sight of soldiers who surrounded the Palace.

I may be permitted to say something about my own qualification to write this history.

I have been connected with the Obrenovich Dynasty during more than thirty years. I have been for a short time private secretary to King Milan, many times Cabinet Minister in several of his Governments, and once the Minister in one of King Alexander's Cabinets (1894), and have had the honour of representing them at several Courts, including four times at the Court of St. James's. For my political career I have to thank principally King Milan, in much smaller measure King Alexander. King Milan was not only my King, but my friend, and I was to him not only a loyal subject, but a devoted friend. To King Alexander I was a loyal subject, but I never was in full sympathy with him, nor he with me, although I liked him very much while he was a delightful little boy, and I can say that little Sasha had so much liking for me that King Milan contemplated for some time entrusting me with the education of the young Prince.

But my devotion to King Milan and my loyalty to King Alexander never made me blind to their shortcomings, mistakes, and insecurity of moral balance. It was, perhaps, my outspokenness and my readiness to tell them always the truth, which secured for me their confidence. My intimate connection with them, coupled with my predilections as an historian —— that is to say, my insistence to discover the truth and without fear to proclaim it, and my permanent desire to be impartial and fair to everyone —— have encouraged me to undertake to write this true story of a great tragedy.

CHEDO MIJATOVICH

LONDON, *June* 11, 1906.

ILLUSTRATIONS

King Milan, Queen Nathalie, and Prince Alexander	83
King Milan and Prince Alexander	84
Prince Alexander	84
King Milan in later life	84
Queen Nathalie	84
King Alexander	85
King Alexander and Queen Draga	85
Wedding procession of King Alexander and Queen Draga	85
Queen Draga	86
Colonel Alexander Mashin	86
Colonel Dragutin Dmitrijevic	86
The royal palace, Belgrade	87
The bodies being thrown from the palace window	87
In Memoriam postcard published after the murders	88
The tomb of the sovereigns, St Mary's Church, Belgrade	88

CHAPTER I

A STRANGE PROPHECY

I wish to write a truthful and impartial history of a young King who was born under extraordinary circumstances, whose childhood was filled with sad events, whose early youth was prematurely darkened by a crown, and who, still a young and inexperienced, although self-willed man, was most cruelly murdered by the very men in whom he placed his trust, and who by a solemn oath were pledged before God and men to serve him faithfully, and die in defence of his life and his honour.

I daresay some readers who have had the patience to read this history attentively to the end will be struck by the similarity of some of its features with Shakespeare's tragedy, *Macbeth*.

I have no wish to increase that similarity, but I cannot resist the temptation to begin my history of a great tragedy in real life with a strange, yet absolutely true, story. It is a contribution to the collection of materials for the solution of the problem: Are human acts and events fore-ordained? and, if so, can they really be foreseen and foretold?

In the spring of the year 1875 the Cabinet Danilo Stefanovich, after repeated fruitless efforts to work with the Skupshtina, decided to dissolve it and have a general election. I was a member of that Cabinet, and it fell to my lot to read in the full House the decree of dissolution.

Although the Constitution clearly reserved the right to the Crown to dissolve the Skupshtina, until that day the dissolution never took place. It was no wonder that the reading of so unexpected a decree made a very deep impression on the members of the Skupshtina. Many of the supporters of the Government came to shake hands with me. The last of them was my friend Mr. Alexa Popovich, a solicitor by profession, and Member for the town of Ujitza, the principal town of the south-western, the most mountainous part of Servia.

"Do you see," he asked me, "how every year brings fresh confirmation of the prophecy of Mata of Kremna? He clearly said that we will have dissolutions of Skupshtinas!"

I told my friend that I did not understand his statement at all. He on his part was surprised that a politician of my position should never have heard anything of the famous political prophecies of the clairvoyant peasant Mata of Kremna. He asked me if Prince Milan knew anything about them, adding, that if the Prince did not, he ought to, as they contained many statements which concerned him personally and his dynasty. Altogether, my friend was not so much impressed by the dissolution of the Skupshtina as by the strange fact that a poor and ignorant peasant should have been able to foretell it some seven years before.

That evening I dined in the Palace with Prince Milan, and after dinner I took an opportunity to tell him what I had heard from Mr. Popovich. As the Prince was very curious, eager, and energetic, he at once called the equerry on duty and ordered him to despatch a letter to Mr. Popovich informing him that he was expected at the Palace early next morning. The Prince told me to come to-morrow at 10 a.m., as he intended receiving the late deputy for Ujitza in my presence.

Next morning before ten o'clock we both were at the Palace. Mr. Popovich, one of the most eloquent men in Servia, told the Prince the story of the clairvoyant peasant in a most graphic, almost picturesque, manner. The story made a deep impression on the young Prince; nor was I less moved. I will give here only the most essential features of the story.

On the 29th May (O.S. = 10th of June N.S.) 1868, about noon, a well-known peasant, by name Mata (Mathews), came in great haste from the neighbouring village of Kremna to the town of Ujitza, and running through the streets cried out loudly and in great alarm: "Oh, brethren! Rise up to help! Save him, save him! They are murdering our Prince! They are cruelly murdering him! Help! Help!"

The police knew Mata as somewhat strange in his manner, but as he talked on that occasion of the murder of the Prince, and as the spreading of false, alarming news was punishable, they, after fruitless endeavours to prevent him shouting, put him under arrest.

Late in the evening of the same day an official telegram from Belgrade announced that Prince Michael Obrenovich III., while walking with his cousin Mme. Anka Constantinovich and her daughter Mile. Katharina in the woods of Koshootnyak (Deer Park), was assassinated. The Prefect of Ujitza, who suspected that Mata of Kremna must have known something about the conspiracy, commenced immediately an interrogatory examination of the poor man. The result of this was that there was no possible connection between the peasant of Kremna and conspirators in Belgrade, but that Mata from time to time had visions of events which are happening at a great distance, or which will happen some day in the nearer or more distant future. That once established, the Prefect invited Mata of Kremna to say what he saw concerning the future, and ordered one of the secretaries to put in writing Mata's statements. According to those "Minutes," or "Proces-Verbal," the clairvoyant of Kremna said:

"Servia will now have a boy for her Prince, but practically the country will be governed by a commission of three persons.

"A few years hence the young boy will be ruler in reality. He is intelligent, but very restless, and will have all sorts of difficulties. The country during his reign will never have rest and repose. He will marry unhappily, will have only one son, will have much trouble with his wife, and at last will divorce her. He will lead several wars, will enlarge the country, will advance in his own station and become a king; but after several years of trouble he will abdicate, go abroad, and die there comparatively young. His son will succeed him, have a still more turbulent and restless reign, will marry a woman from the people, and in his twenty-seventh or twenty-eighth year will cease to be king, his dynasty perishing with him. He will be replaced on the throne by Peter Karageorgevich, who will reign about three years and then also disappear. A foreign army will enter the country, and the people will suffer very much. At last a man will arise from the midst of the people, will drive away the foreigners, unite all the Servian people under his reign, and inaugurate a happy era of national history."

I have not myself read those Minutes, and mention here the essential points such as I heard them for the first time in the Palace of Belgrade in the presence of Prince Milan, from a man who has seen and read the prophecies of Mata of Kremna, written by a secretary in the presence of the Prefect of Ujitza.

* * * * * * *

On the 19th of February (O.S. = 3rd March N.S.) 1889, King Milan communicated to the President of his Cabinet, Mr. Nicholas Christich, that he had firmly resolved to abdicate on the 22nd of February, the Servian national festival. All the Ministers went together to the Palace to try to persuade the King to abandon such an unworthy and fatal intention. We spent nearly two hours in trying to open his eyes to the inevitable and the mischievous consequences of such a step. At last King Milan said to us: "Gentlemen, you certainly have done your duty, you have brought before me all the possible arguments against my abdication, most of which arguments I cannot dispute. You are right, but in spite of all that and everything else, I cannot do otherwise! Nothing can shake me in my determination! Let me add, that I do not wonder at your insistence, but I do wonder that Mijatovich excites himself into a rage against my abdication, when he knows well that it must take place."

The moment we left Queen Nathalie's boudoir (where our interview with King Milan took place) our President begged us all to come to his office to a sort of informal Cabinet meeting. Hardly had we taken our chairs around him, when the old gentleman in his earnest, quiet, and dignified manner addressed us —

"Gentlemen, you all heard the King say that our colleague, Mr. Mijatovich, knew well that the abdication must take place! As none of us knew anything about it, I think we have the right to ask our colleague for an explanation: why, knowing that the abdication would take place, he never told us?"

I assured the President and my colleagues that I was absolutely ignorant of the King's intention of abdicating now; that I had only a few days ago, in answer to a confidential question put to me by the British Minister, assured His Excellency that his German colleague, Count Bray, was quite wrong when he told him that the King was going to abdicate in a few days, for the King had certainly no intention to abdicate now, although that might be the case in four years, when his son comes of age.

This assurance was well received by my colleagues, but the President did not let me escape. "But, then, how do you explain His Majesty's words?" he asked me again.

"Very simply," I answered. "Many years ago the King and I heard at the same time, and for the first time, the details of the prophecy of Mata of Kremna, where it was mentioned that he would abdicate and leave the country." And I told them then all I knew about Mata's prophecy.

Some of my colleagues protested that I was joking in such a crisis, others laughed at the stupidity of an explanation apparently invented at random.

But the old "Uncle Nicholas" (*Chicha Nikola*, as we lovingly called our highly respected President), came most unexpectedly to my assistance.

"Gentlemen," he began, "our colleague's explanation may seem to you strange, but I for my part have not the slightest doubt that it is perfectly true. You remember that I had the misfortune to be the Home Minister at the time of Prince Michael's assassination. I recollect that the Prefect of Ujitza reported to me on the remarkable statements of the clairvoyant peasant. I gave orders that the original document, on which his statements were written, should be sent to me. I have read it myself, and I think it could be found now, among the secret papers of the year 1868, in this very building."

I might give to my readers yet a few interesting details from that very remarkable political prophecy of a poor and ignorant Servian peasant; but I refrain, because in a later chapter I will, at Queen Draga's interview with a loyal friend only a few days before her assassination, report their conversation on that very prophecy. I will say here only that all the principal events of Servian history during the last thirty years (since I knew something about Mata's prognostication) have remarkably agreed with what he told the Prefect of Ujitza and his secretary in the year 1868.

CHAPTER II

THE BIRTH OF KING ALEXANDER

In the month of May 1874, Prince Milan Obrenovich IV of Servia surprised his Government and his people by announcing to them in an open telegram from Vienna that he had become engaged to Mademoiselle Nathalie Kechko. This came as an unwelcome surprise to the Ministers, who had been planning to obtain for him the hand of one of several young Russian Princesses; in fact the President of his Cabinet, Yovan Marinovich, at that time one of the favourites of the Russian Government, already had made confidential advances in that direction in St. Petersburg. At the same time, however, unknown to the Government, Milan's mother, Princess Helene Obrenovich, *née* Catargi, had selected a bride for her son. By her arrangement Princess Mourousi, the aunt and the guardian of the young children of her deceased sister Mme. Kechko, brought her niece Nathalie to Vienna. Milan was invited to Vienna to see the young lady. The moment he saw her he fell passionately in love with her. She was then hardly eighteen, and very pretty. Her large, dark, and very expressive eyes, together with her brilliant complexion and somewhat Armenian, if not Georgian, cast of countenance, gave her the stamp of an Oriental beauty. No one could come into her presence without feeling that she was the type of a superior woman. Struck from the first moment by her beauty, Prince Milan was soon fascinated by her spiritual qualities. In his first conversation with her he found that this Oriental beauty had the culture of an Occidental lady, and more especially that she had the brilliant *esprit* of a Frenchwoman.

    I saw King Milan on his return from the interview with his bride in Vienna. I also saw him frequently during the first and second year of his wedded life, and I do not hesitate to say that he was deeply, sincerely, and honestly in love with his wife.

The Servians at that time were devoted to their young sovereign, and, because of that devotion, they were bitterly disappointed that he did not marry a Russian Princess. Besides, everyone asked, "Who are the Kechkos?" All that could be said in reply was that Nathalie's parents belonged to the old Moldavian nobility, that they had large estates in Bessarabia, and that her father died Colonel of one of the Russian Cavalry regiments. Rumours were soon current that people who knew well the Kechko family rather doubted that King Milan had made a happy choice. The disappointment spread and deepened, nor could it be lessened by the exaggerated stories of the Kechkos' great wealth. But when, at the request of Prince Milan, Prince and Princess Mourousi and their niece Nathalie, on their return from Vienna to Moldavia, travelling by steamer down the Danube, stopped at Belgrade, and the affianced young couple drove in an open carriage through the thronged streets of the capital of Servia, Nathalie at once won the hearts of all by her beauty, modesty, and childlike simplicity. I myself was present at that first reception of the future Queen in Belgrade, and I never before heard or saw the Servians so spontaneously and so genuinely enthusiastic as on that occasion. The young Prince Milan was radiant with happiness at the reception his capital gave his engaged bride. Probably that was the happiest day in the lives of both Milan and Nathalie. Even those who knew something of the prophecy of the Kremna clairvoyant, as I did, did not believe that it could ever be possible that these two young people, so handsome, so intelligent, so in love with each other, and so enthusiastically greeted by a gifted and affectionate people, could ever persecute each other with a relentless and cruel hatred.

The wedding took place in Belgrade Cathedral, on 9th October, under somewhat difficult circumstances. Just before the arrival of the bride in Belgrade for the ceremony, a Cabinet crisis took place, and Prince Milan had great difficulty in forming a new one. Indeed, the wedding had to be postponed for a few days until the Prince succeeded in doing so. It then took place amidst great rejoicings, and the genuine enthusiasm of the people. The joyfulness of the occasion was increased by the Tzar having consented to act, through a special envoy, as the "Koom" to the young couple. The "Koom" at a Servian wedding is the principal witness, the best man and something more than that; he is in a sense the protector of the couple, their trustee, their best and most respected friend through life. The Servians, who are almost all Russophil, and worshippers of the Tzar, felt very much flattered that the ruler of the mighty and "invincible" Russia should become the "Koom" of their young Prince and Princess.

Curiously, a few insignificant incidents were regarded by the superstitious people of Belgrade as bad omens.

After the ceremony in the Cathedral, and when the newly-wedded, young princely couple had taken their places in the open carriage to return to the Palace, the horses at first refused to move from the spot. Urged on by the grooms and watchmen, they began to rear, and for a few moments there was a danger that the carriage with the bride and bridegroom would be overturned!

Another incident, which the people considered of evil portent, was that hardly had the young Prince and his bride, with their suite, reached the Palace, when a brief but violent storm burst over the town. I remember distinctly that in the great Hall of the Palace, where the State dignitaries and their wives were assembled to congratulate the bride and bridegroom, and just when the young couple entered the Hall, the thick clouds of the storm caused such a darkness that we could hardly see each other, as at that time there was neither gas nor electric light in the Palace. A high dignitary, a friend of mine and a devoted friend of the dynasty, who was standing near me, after a suppressed involuntary exclamation whispered to me, "Dost thou not notice the remarkable resemblance between the head of the Princess and the head of a tigress?" It was then for me to utter a suppressed exclamation of painful surprise.

In later years, or rather, in the sad and dark years of the divorce, King Milan on several occasions said to me, "You all, who know Nathalie from a distance, have nothing but adoration for her, but *I* know how cruel she can be!"

✻ ✻ ✻ ✻ ✻ ✻ ✻

The newly-married couple had no "honeymoon." The Prince could not absent himself for even a day or two. The excitement in the country was growing more dangerous every day. The Liberal press of Servia, abetted and inspired by the Slavophils of Russia, clamoured for war against Turkey. Prince Milan knew well that Servia was not prepared for a war, either with regard to armament or financially. The rumours that he was personally opposed to it made him lose his popularity in certain military and political circles. The friends of Peter Karageorgevich began at once to exploit the situation. The stories of the military genius of Kara-George were revived and spread, especially among the officers and young politicians already heated by the daily clamour of the Liberal press (practically the Slavophil press): "War with Turkey! now or never!" Also, the news of the personal bravery of Prince Peter, who under the name of a famous national hero of old time, Mrkonich, had joined the Servian insurgents of Bosnia, was widely circulated among the people, with comments that if Milan Obrenovich had not the courage or capacity to lead the Servians against the Turks, Peter Karageorgevich would have both. The Russian Slavophils, whose aim was to force the peace-loving Tzar Alexander n. into war with Turkey, hoped to succeed by pushing forward Servia and Montenegro as a sort of Russian advance-guard; on this account they attempted to utilise the anti-dynastic elements of Servia to intimidate Prince Milan into placing himself at their service. As I was well known as a personal friend of the Prince, several officers asked me to inform him that the only chance to prevent an anti-dynastic revolution was that Obrenovich IV. should at once lead the Servian Army against the Turks, and not leave that truly national and noble task to Peter Karageorgevich. But young Milan met all such reports by an answer which for some time at least was stereotyped: —

"Do you expect me to try to save the dynasty by leading the nation into a war which must inevitably end by our defeat on the battlefield? Neither could our artillery cope with the Turkish artillery, nor could our National Army (the militia) successfully fight with the Turkish regular troops. By a war with Turkey in our present state we would simply march deliberately towards a catastrophe!"

The uncertainty of the situation, and the young Prince's and Princess's resulting anxiety and perplexity, were materially increased by the equivocal conduct of Russia. Prince Gortchakoff repeatedly and officially advised Prince Milan and his Government that they ought by all means preserve the peace, and carefully avoid everything that could provoke a Turkish attack on Servia; and that the Prince would incur the personal displeasure of the Tzar if he should disregard His Imperial Majesty's advice in this respect, given in the interest of Servia as well as that of the general peace. At the same time confidential but urgent advices came from the Russian Ambassador in Constantinople, General Ignyatieff, that in the interest of Servia, and of the whole

Slavonic world, Servia should not hesitate longer, but should declare war on Turkey at once!

Prince Milan, although not exactly a Slavophil, was a sincere Russophil, and his Premier, Mr. Yovan Ristich, was not only a Russophil, but very largely, although not entirely, a Slavophil. Mr. Ristich, who was an experienced statesman, and knew well the methods of the Russian policy, persuaded the Prince that the real mind of Russia and the Tzar was that expressed in Ignyatieff's confidential communications, and that Gortchakoff's telegrams were only practically addressed to the gallery of "Dame Europe," and were not expected to be taken literally by Servia. I believe the Prince must have received assurances from Russia, that even if his fears of Servian defeat should be unfortunately realised, neither Servia nor the Obrenovich Dynasty would experience unfavourable consequences by such a defeat. At any rate Prince Milan declared war on Turkey on the 18th June 1876.

I am reviewing, as briefly as possible, the political situation of Servia during the time intervening between the marriage of Milan and Nathalie and the declaration of war against Turkey, simply as an indication of the exciting and anxious circumstances in which the young Princess Nathalie was expecting her first confinement. Would it be extraordinary if the great and almost permanent tension of nerves under which the young mother lived all those months had affected the nervous constitution of her first boy?

* * * * * * *

At the end of the first six weeks of the war, no important action had as yet taken place. In truth the war was not popular with the Servian peasantry. I have seen thousands of militia pass the barracks of Kralyevo (where I had installed my offices and stores as Intendant of the I bar corps), all looking earnest and gloomy. I hardly ever heard anyone sing a patriotic song, or cheer. The individual bravery of the Turks and the greatness of the Turkish Empire caused the majority of the militia to feel that we had no chance against the Sultan. The gloom was spreading to the intelligent class too, because we all expected that, immediately after our declaration of war, the Christians in general, and the Servians more particularly, would enthusiastically rise in a general insurrection against Turkey in Old Servia and in

Macedonia. But to our great astonishment, and utter disgust, not a man rose in those provinces!

Each day our depression was increased by our anxiety as to what the next day would bring, as a general attack by the Turkish army was now daily expected. Early in the morning of the 14th August (the 2nd August according to the O.S.) a telegram from Krushevatz announced to our office that from the east great cannonading was heard, and that the peasants just arrived from Moravia were stating that from early dawn the firing of cannon had been heard in the distance all along the fortification line from Gyunis to Deligrad. A quarter of an hour later the cannon of a battery, which was temporarily in Kralyevo, began to fire, and the Prefect of the Canton came to show me the telegram from the Prefect of Chachak announcing the happy confinement of the Princess of a healthy boy! This was announced to the citizens of the small, but pretty and clean town of Kralyevo by a drummer (a sort of town-crier), and they immediately decorated their houses with national flags, shut their shops for the day, and brought out barrels of wine and beer to the central square, for free distribution to the soldiers and militiamen and every man willing to drink to the health and happiness of the new-born heir to the throne of Servia. On that day Servia had nearly a hundred thousand men under arms at different strategic points, and they all abandoned their depression and gloom, and heartily cheered the news that the Prince and Princess had a son, and the country an heir to the throne. The officers in all the camps drank heartily to the health of the boy, whom they declared to have been born on a battlefield, and whom they hoped would prove to be a grand soldier and a great leader of men, a new Dooshan,[1] predestined to unite all the Servian provinces into one kingdom. Even the superstitious Servian peasant was pleased, because he considered the birth of an heir to their sovereign just then as a good omen of Servian victory over the Turks. I do not exaggerate when I say that, excepting a handful of Prince Karageorgevich's partisans, the vast majority of the Servians greeted with a sincere joy and with their best wishes the birth of Obrenovich the Fifth, to whom his god-father, Tzar Alexander II., gave, through his representative at baptism, his own name Alexander. Is it not a strange fact, that Alexander the god-father and Alexander the god-son, both died by a violent and terrible death?

1 Dooshan is the name of the greatest Servian ruler in the Middle Ages.

CHAPTER III

SASHA'S CHILDHOOD

Queen Nathalie loved Servia and the Servian people with all the enthusiasm of a young, highly intelligent, and warm-hearted woman. She very quickly developed into a true Servian patriot. But, as she herself used always to say, "in her innermost heart she never ceased to be a Russian, and loved Russia probably, and at least, as well as she loved Servia."

It was quite natural that she should call her boy "Sasha," which is the Russian endearing and caressing diminutive for Alexander. The future King Alexander was always to his mother and father, their relatives, to the intimate friends of the dynasty, as well as, later on, to his own sweetheart and wife Draga, nothing but Sasha. Queen Nathalie's beautiful villa in Biarritz bears to this day the name "Sashino," which means "Sasha's Villa."

King Alexander was not quite twenty-seven years old when he was murdered. Of these twenty-seven years of his life the first nine years only of his childhood were something like happy years. Even his early youth was not quite normal; he was practically a lonely boy, his parents having no other children, and there being no aristocracy and no really superior class of society in Servia, the young boy had no companions and playmates, but was always surrounded by grown-up people. Yet the poor little boy, from amongst more or less polished officers of the Court and grey-bearded, serious-looking statesmen and politicians, who filled the ante-chamber of the Konak, looked quite happy with his fresh complexion and dark eyes like those of his mother. And more especially he looked happy if he was able to commit some practical joke on his grown-up entourage. He was very intelligent, but a most restless and mischievous boy, and exceedingly wilful. Queen Nathalie and his first governess, Mademoiselle Pellingre (a Swiss lady of Geneva), had hard work with his education. He learned very easily and quickly, had a wonderful memory, astounded everybody with his logical reasoning and his arithmetical and mathematical proclivities, but he rebelled against discipline and all regulations. His restlessness and mischievousness, as well as his bad teeth, made Queen Nathalie sometimes despair.

I will illustrate with one or two examples what a young rogue the little Sasha was.

On one occasion King Milan with the Queen and the little Sasha were travelling by steamer up the river Sava to visit the prosperous town of Shabatz. The well-to-do citizens hired three steamers and came to meet the Royal party at some distance from the town. The steamers were slowly and very closely passing the Royal steamer, the citizens cheering enthusiastically the little Sasha, whom I was holding on a chair in front of me. "Why do they shout so much?" the boy asked, who never before heard a cheering crowd. "Because they love you!" I told him. Then, to my astonishment, he raised his voice and shouted to the citizens crowding the steamers: "Mijatovich says you love me! If it is true that you love me, throw, all of you, your hats into the water!" And the loyal and good citizens of Shabatz threw their hats into the river, cheering most enthusiastically. King Milan was amused, and laughed, but Queen Nathalie was greatly annoyed, and reprimanded the mischievous Sasha very sharply before all his cheering friends.

On the same occasion he took my right glove and threw it into the river, saying to me, "You know some fish may also want to have gloves!" Queen Nathalie told him in a very severe tone that he would have to be punished for mischief-making. A quarter of an hour later he managed to get my left glove too, and threw it into the river. The Queen, quite flushed with annoyance, angrily said, "Sasha, for this new misdeed your first punishment will be to-night trebled." "But, mamma," said the little boy very quickly, "that would not be right! You were right to punish me for my throwing Mr. Mijatovich's right glove to the fishes, but why punish me when I throw his left glove, which is no value to him without the right one?"

Once when Sasha was in his tenth year he rushed into the great Hall of the Palace, not knowing that the King and Queen were receiving there a great deputation of the National Assembly. The Queen beckoned to him to come to her, and he did so, standing in front of her. He listened quietly for some time, but as King Milan's eloquence flowed on continually without stopping, the boy became restless and looked how he could escape. The Queen bent over him and whispered to him somewhat audibly, "Sasha, keep quiet, or another time we shall not let you be with us when we receive deputations!" Whereupon the little boy, in the hearing of all, replied, "Do you think, mamma, I shall be such a fool as to come again to listen to the long speeches of papa? Not I!" King Milan was the first to laugh heartily, finishing in that way his speech to the deputies, who cheered lustily, probably more for the spirited boy than his eloquent papa. I was present on the occasion.

To be absolutely impartial I must tell another incident which seemed to me at the time it happened very characteristic, and which affected me sadly. On the return of King Milan from a foreign voyage in 1882, when he was entering the Belgrade Cathedral a woman fired two shots at him from a revolver. Although the King was not wounded there was great excitement in the town and at the Palace. The little Sasha, far more curious and inquisitive than the average boy of six years generally is, tried to find out what was really the cause for so much commotion in the Palace as well as in the streets. At last he rushed to his particular friend, General Tesha Nicolich, the War Minister. That giant among the Servian officers, always a jolly and jovial fellow, took the little boy on his knee and laughingly told him how a foolish woman tried to kill his papa. The poor little Sasha wept bitter tears because anyone wanted to kill his good papa. I approached him, and helped the General to quiet the grief of the boy. Then suddenly the boy's face was transfigured. He stopped crying, looked pale and trembling, jumped down from the General's knee, and in a great anger said to him, "Tesha, go at once with your soldiers and catch that wicked woman, and with your own sword cut her into pieces, and throw them into that deep well in our garden!" General Tesha laughed heartily, but I was dumbfounded, and wondered at such an explosion of cruelty in a little boy. In after years whenever I heard King Alexander use a cruel word I invariably remembered this incident of 1882.

But on the whole, during the first nine years of his life Sasha was a charming and most affectionate boy.

With the very beginning of the second period of nine years of the short and sad life of Alexander Obrenovich, dark clouds began to overshadow his young heart. Affectionately loving both his father and his mother, he suddenly found himself between them the kicking ball of their mutual hatred. How it came about that Milan and Nathalie, who married from love at first sight, transformed their mutual love into the most uncompromising hatred I do not intend to tell here. It would complicate the great tragedy by another, not so terrible, but sad, very sad, in which neither of his parents played consistently a noble part. Perhaps the most dramatic element in the Milan-Nathalie tragedy was the assertion of each party that they loved their boy. Because of his devoted love for his boy King Milan moved heaven and earth to take him away from the arms of his mother; while Queen Nathalie professed that because she was an intensely loving mother she could not bear the separation from her most beloved and only boy Sasha. They preferred to fight a most ignominious fight before the eyes of the world, and before the eyes of their utterly distracted and despairing little boy. Queen Nathalie refused to return the boy to his father, the heir to the throne of Servia. King Milan did not hesitate to appeal to the German policy, and the German policemen had to enter the apartments of Queen Nathalie and take by force from her arms the poor, bitterly weeping boy. This scandal, created by Milan and Nathalie in Wiesbaden, resounded from one end of the world to the other. It was painful and humiliating enough, and it would be no wonder if it had then and there eradicated every affection for his parents from the young heart of the boy.

Then came the second and somewhat protracted scandal. King Milan demanded from the Servian Church to be divorced from Queen Nathalie. Everybody in Servia knew well that Queen Nathalie was an absolutely virtuous woman, and Milan neither did nor could reproach her for incontinence. The incompatibility of temper which he practically invoked was not a valid reason for divorce in the Greek Orthodox Church. His action for divorce was first started before the ordinary ecclesiastic Church. But when it was seen that the regular procedure might last a whole year, keeping all that time the scandal before the people of Servia, who began to show some signs of impatience, then it was necessary to hunt for some precedents in the old Byzantine Empire and in Russia. In the last country it was found that the Tzars had been sometimes divorced by the simple edict (Grammota) of the Metropolitan, and, following such precedents in the "Holy Orthodox Russia," the Archbishop Theodosius, the Primate of Servia, declared the marriage bond between King Milan and Queen Nathalie dissolved.

These proceedings, lasting from June to the middle of September 1888, had paralysed the political life of Servia and disorganised the great party of Obrenovich, strengthening at the same time and encouraging the partisans of the Pretender Karageorgevich. Russia, hating King Milan as a sort of deserter and traitor of the "Slavonic Cause," utilised the general dissatisfaction of the people with the King's divorce, and organised in Europe, and more especially in Servia, a regular campaign of the most unscrupulous calumnies against King Milan. At the same time the mistress of the King, Mme. Arthemise Christich, always suspected to have been a secret agent of Russia, began to suggest to King Milan to abdicate.

The idea of abdication was cleverly counselled him by his mistress immediately after the first difficulties encountered with the regular ecclesiastical court of divorces. Passing through Vienna on his way to Gleichenberg (the famous watering-place for lung diseases near Gratz in Styria) in the beginning of July 1888, he communicated his intention to some intimate friends in the Austrian capital. As Minister for Foreign Affairs in Mr. Nicholas Christich's Cabinet, I received confidential information, and wrote at once a very outspoken letter to King Milan, showing him plainly the cowardliness of such an act, and the great sin which he would commit against his son if he were to pass the crown to the boy, as his education had been hardly begun. The King invited me to come at once to Gleichenberg. There for five days I argued against his fatal idea of abdication. My appeal to him on behalf of his son did not produce much effect. To one of such arguments he said: "You know my Sasha is to me by far the dearest creature in the world, yet from time to time he seems to me a sort of disguised personification of his mother. He has sometimes her cold, cruel laugh." I made on him more impression by showing him that to descend from the throne at that particular time, when his own actions gave to his wife and to Russia the opportunity to represent him in the European press as the meanest of men, would be his moral suicide for all time. I suggested to him to postpone his abdication until his son came of age, in five years, and use that time to give his son a solid preparation for his position, educate him as the future King of Servia ought to be educated, and at the same time doing good to his people, so that he would regain his somewhat tarnished popularity in Servia, and re-establish his own good reputation in Europe, which certain newspapers in Austria, Germany, and France, paid by Russia, had seriously compromised. I drew up for him a programme of what he could and ought to do, the first article being that now, when nobody in Servia hopes to get a better and more liberal Constitution, he should by his own personal initiative grant the nation a truly liberal and well-considered Constitution. He seemed to be much impressed, and led me to believe that he accepted it entirely and in all its details. In reality he executed only the first article, and instead of abdicating in 1897 he abdicated on the 22nd February 1889.

Sasha was in the middle of his thirteenth year when he was proclaimed King of Servia (12 years 6 months and 20 days). We Servians are rather superstitious people, and I know many friends of the dynasty Obrenovich who considered it an evil omen that King Alexander ascended the throne of Servia in his thirteenth year. The extraordinary calmness, self-possession, and dignity with which the boy conducted himself on that memorable day on which he was by his own father proclaimed, in the White Hall of the New Palace, King of Servia, was very much appreciated. No one admired him more than his own father. No one less than I personally. It seemed to me so unnatural that this boy of twelve and a half years, surrounded by the civil State dignitaries and higher officers all deeply moved, most of them in tears and loudly sobbing, his own father kneeling before him pronouncing the oath of fidelity as subject to his new King, should not betray the slightest emotion! Has he a heart? Has he nerves? No, this was evidently not an ordinary boy.

I left the Palace deeply saddened. I felt strongly that my adored King Milan had committed a terrible and fatal mistake. And I was puzzled about that cold face of the boy King. I tried to explain it. The public, acrimonious, and most unscrupulous struggle of his parents, and the scandal of their divorce, how could they but fill the young heart of this boy with shame and bitterness? They certainly could not plant, and much less develop, noble sentiments in his heart. The permanence and the growth of the anti-dynastic movement, the incessant precautions under which the Royal Court had to live, the intrigues of the foreign Powers, what influence could they exercise on the young boy's character, whose sharp and intelligent eyes they did not escape? Nothing but the most pernicious influence. Nor did I forget that Dr. Dokich, to whose educational care Sasha since his seventh year was entrusted, although an able physician and scientist, and a man of high morality, practically was an atheist, whose principal and almost exclusive anxiety was to keep the boy in good physical health and to give him a certain amount of scientific information. No one took care for his religious and moral education. The Court Chaplain, Prota Yacov (who will later on, as Archbishop Inokentiye, bless the murderers of King Alexander), succeeded only in making religion an object for witty observations and awkward questions on the part of his Royal pupil. And his own parents, would they have persecuted each other with such a persistent and unscrupulous hatred as they did, if they had cared better for his moral education, for the development of all that was noble and good, and for the suppression of all that was mean and bad? The unfortunate boy, who became King in his thirteenth year, passed the last three years of his childhood under most demoralising and sad circumstances. There could be no wonder that on the first, the most solemn and most emotional, occasion he appeared as King, he looked as if he had been made of cold marble and not of flesh and blood, a boy in his thirteenth year!

CHAPTER IV

THE SILENT BOY KING

The circumstances in which the so-called "education" of the young King Alexander was pursued, were most depressing.

Having decided to leave his son and his country, King Milan's great study was how to prevent Queen Nathalie exercising any influence on his son and his country. It seems that before he appointed Mr. Yovan Ristich, General Yotza Belimarkovich, and General Kosta Protich the Regents of the Kingdom during King Alexander's minority, King Milan exacted from them a promise that on no account would they allow Queen Nathalie to have the slightest influence on the education of her son, the young King. He delivered his son to them on the condition that they should become a safe and solid barrier, closing every approach by which Queen Nathalie could reach her son. On that understanding he was ready to separate himself from his son and go into voluntary exile. He loved his son and loved his country, but was willing to put himself under the permanent torture of living away from them if he could prevent Nathalie being with her son! King Milan was not a cruel man, but to his divorced wife he behaved often with cruelty. Queen Nathalie, on her part, would gladly undergo any torture if she only could thereby inflict suffering and humiliation on King Milan. These two otherwise highly intelligent people continued their cruel struggle against each other under the eyes of their young boy, without giving a moment's consideration to the fact that to him their behaviour was most cruel.

It is, of course, charitable to suppose that Queen Nathalie's motives for her action were in the first place her motherly love for her son, and the sentiment of her maternal duty towards him. But this sentiment of duty was made the more imperative by the sweet consideration that the fulfilment of her duty towards her son would cause annoyance and humiliation to her hated husband, Milan.

She decided to come to Belgrade and take her position in the Palace as the mother of the King. She came to Belgrade, but only to find that, at the order of the Regents, all the gates of the Palace had been closed to her. The young boy King could see from one of the windows of the Palace how his mother had to turn away from its closed gates, scrutinising eagerly every window of the old Konak in the hope of seeing the face of her boy. It was indeed cruel. The Regents informed the mother of their King that she would not be allowed to enter the Palace, nor speak to her son, nor keep up a correspondence with him. The same cruel programme was enjoined on the young King, and all his teachers, professors, equerries, and servants were ordered to co-operate in its strict execution. The Queen was advised, and politely requested by the Regents and their Government, to leave Belgrade. She refused to do so. She hired a house in the immediate neighbourhood of the Palace, a house past which the young King, surrounded by guards, drove every day, so that his unfortunate mother could from time to time catch a glimpse of his face.

If the imagination of a sensational novelist had created such a tragic situation, his readers would say that such a situation was impossible in real life. Yet here was a woman, and a queen too, young, beautiful, high-spirited, loving passionately and hating passionately, watching eagerly every day from the window of a one-storeyed and inconvenient house (once belonging to Princess Persida Karageorgevich, the mother of King Peter!) to catch a glimpse of her only boy! And there was that poor boy, surrounded by more or less rough horsemen, throwing silently his sad glance towards the windows, that he might get, perchance, a glimpse of his mother! The Regents thought they were behaving like gentlemen by keeping their promise to King Milan. In reality they were daily putting under agony the heart of a mother, perhaps also the heart of a boy! The young boy King was sad and silent. No one knew what was passing in his young soul. But every student of human nature must feel that that extraordinary situation could not, from an educational point of view, otherwise but disastrously influence the formation of character of the young boy King.

This condition of affairs could not go on indefinitely for those principally concerned in it. The Regents were first to find the tragedy unbearable. They considered how to end it as speedily as possible.

They hit upon an extraordinary plan. Who was the originator I do not know. Some believe it was the fertile brain of King Milan, who was ready to humiliate himself if he could only revenge himself on his divorced wife. Others, again, believe the plan originated with the Russian Government, which would not hesitate to sacrifice Queen Nathalie, so faithful and devoted to Russia, if only the gates of Servia were shut and securely bolted against Russia's *bête noire*, King Milan. Anyhow, a Bill was brought into the National Assembly proposing that neither King Milan, the father of His Majesty King Alexander, nor Queen Nathalie, the mother of His Majesty, should be allowed to reside even temporarily in Servia, and once out of the country they should never be permitted to re-enter it again. The Radical majority of the National Assembly, permeated as it was by friends and agents of the Pretender, voted with enthusiasm the expulsion of King Milan and Queen Nathalie for ever from Servia!

It was the second great blow to the foundations of the Obrenovich Dynasty. Who would have respect for the helpless boy on the throne when his gifted father, who made Servia an independent kingdom with largely increased territory, and his once so highly and justly popular mother, are expelled and forbidden to enter the country to which they both were sincerely and fervently devoted? The law was a monument of the ingratitude of the people. It was unjust and cruel to King Milan and to Queen Nathalie, and still more unjust and cruel to the boy King Alexander. Was that the lesson of generosity and of largeness of heart which Servia was giving to her young King? Did not the Regents, their Government, and the Skupshtina act as if they expected that the poor boy, who had the misfortune to be their King, should mortify all his love for his father and mother? Did they not teach him to behave like an unnatural boy? Did no one consider what a dangerous education they were giving to their young King?

Immediately after the resolution was passed by the National Assembly, the Government requested Queen Nathalie to leave Belgrade. On her refusal to do so, a police commissioner, with several armed policemen, were ordered to take her by force to one of the steamers plying every half-hour between Belgrade and the Hungarian frontier-town, Zimony. As the great and heavy gate of the house in which Queen Nathalie lived was closed and barred, the police commissioner and his men had to climb from the neighbouring yards over the walls into the yard of the Queen's temporary home. When the police force reached her private sitting-room, Queen Nathalie protested against the violent and illegal action of the Government, but at the same time declared she was ready to yield to their violence. A common and dirty cab was called, and the proud Queen Nathalie had to take her seat in it at the side of the personally most distressed police commissioner, and with a fully-armed gendarme on the seat near the coachman.

The cab passed the Palace. Did poor Sasha witness the humiliation of his queenly mother? I do not know; but he certainly was at that time in the Palace.

Crowds of the people gathered in the principal streets leading to the steamer's pier. Their natural and general sentiment was that their headstrong and imperious Queen had been harshly and undeservedly treated. Suddenly a group of young men stopped the cab, drove away the police commissioner and the police, as well as the cabman, took out the horses, turned the carriage, and dragged it, with Queen Nathalie in tears from deep emotion, back to her house, through the principal streets of Belgrade, and past the Palace of her boy. Dense crowds of men and women followed her, enthusiastically cheering. If poor Sasha did not see half an hour earlier the humiliation of his mother, he must have seen, attracted by the incessant cheers of the crowds, her triumph.

A few moments after she reached her house, several companies of soldiers and gendarmes summoned the dense crowd in front of the house to disperse. When the people refused to do so the soldiers fired, killing a few young men and wounding many. Queen Nathalie then induced the people to disperse, telling them that to prevent further bloodshed she would of her own will leave Belgrade. This she did the same evening.

What a day for the poor mother of the boy King! What a day for Servia, and especially what a day for the boy King himself! Is it possible that such a day has not exercised a deep impression on the mind and heart of the young boy, filling it with contempt, bitterness, and hatred? All the action of the Regents, their Government, their National Assembly, and the police, was fundamentally wrong, and indeed immoral. How can it be expected that such action should favourably influence the moral education of the boy King?

In my opinion, he was at that time decidedly more sinned against than sinning.

CHAPTER V

HOW THE SILENT SASHA BECAME "ALEXANDER THE GREAT"

In the preceding chapter I mentioned those dramatic and tragic events, the resolution of the National Assembly forbidding the parents of King Alexander to sojourn in Servia, and the terrible expulsion of Queen Nathalie from Belgrade, which demoralised the Obrenovich Party and weakened the position of the dynasty in Servia. I allowed readers themselves to conjecture the pernicious influence those sad events must have exercised on the character of the young boy King Alexander.

Further political developments worked fatally in the same direction. The Regency was composed of at least two very strong Liberals (Ristich and Belimarkovich), even if we admit that General Protich, the third Regent, did not formally belong to the Liberal Party, although practically he shared their opinion and their programme. The Liberals have since the restoration of the dynasty of Obrenovich in 1859 always boasted that they were the true dynastic party. The Radicals followed blindly the leaders, who were always bitter opponents of the Obrenovich, and who were more than suspected of working for the restoration of the Karageorgevich Dynasty. The Liberal Regency and the Radical Government were obliged to carry on the legislation and the administration of the country; but they were watching each other with great misgivings and suspicion. I know as a positive fact that the Regents feared that their own Radical Government, having so successfully "buried alive King Milan and Queen Nathalie," might one night by a *coup de main* arrest the Regents, kill or carry out of the country the young King Alexander, and proclaim King Peter Karageorgevich King of Servia. The Radicals, although they had an enormous majority in the Assembly, and practically had the administration of the country in their hands, felt keenly that so long as the Liberals, through the Regents, exercised practically the Royal power, they were not the masters of the situation as they ought and wished to be, and from the very beginning of the Regency the struggle for supremacy between the Radicals and Liberals went on, although both sides were anxious for the time being to save appearances.

But something unexpected then happened which forced upon the country a real political crisis. The third Regent, General Kosta Protich died suddenly in June 1891. Immediately the Radicals declared that his place in the Regency must be taken by their leader, Mr. Nichola Pashich. The two Regents, Ristich and Belimarkovich, considered it their duty to prevent the election of a Radical as the third Regent. The Radical Government insisted that the National Assembly should be convoked at once, to elect the third Regent. The Regents thought differently. To exercise pressure on the Regency the Radical Government placed it in the dilemma, either of summoning at once the Assembly for the purpose of electing the third Regent, or accepting their resignation. The Regents, to the utter astonishment of the Radicals, accepted their resignation, and requested Mr. Avakumovich to form a Liberal Cabinet.

Then began a violent and passionate struggle between the Liberals and the Radicals. The latter had undoubtedly a great majority in the country, especially among the peasants; but the Liberals had the administration of the country in their hands. They dissolved the Radical Skupshtina, replaced the Radical Prefects, and other influential employés of the State, by experienced and energetic Liberals, who exercised all sorts of influences to secure the election of Liberals as Presidents of village communities, and after this preparatory work of several months undertook the general election for the new Skupshtina. The Radicals were better organised. They were fortunate enough to have the majority of the village priests and village teachers for their partisans, and these proved most active and energetic agents. Both parties did not hesitate in the choice of means to secure victory at the election. The Radicals described the Liberal Regents and the Liberal Ministers as old enemies of the national liberties, who desired to place the people under the heel of the Chinovniks, that these might oppress them, and increase taxation to fill their own pockets. The Liberals described the Radicals as the sworn enemies of the Obrenovich Dynasty, which had done such signal service to the country, and hinted that all those who voted for the Radicals would be named in the police registers as men suspected of the anti-dynastic sentiment, and treated by the State authorities as such. There is no doubt that in their anxiety to secure a majority, the police authorities exercised in some places brutal pressure on the electors. One place in the Canton of Dragachevo (notorious for its opposition to the rulers of the Obrenovich Dynasty) came to an open riot, to suppress which the police called soldiers to their aid, and caused some bloodshed.

But in spite of the reckless energy of the Liberal Government, the number of the Liberal members hardly balanced the number of the Radical members. In normal circumstances the Government ought to have resigned. But the Liberals persuaded themselves that the interest of the dynasty, as well as the interest of the State, demanded more than ever that they should hold office. They decided to annul several Radical elections, and put the Liberals in their places, regardless of the illegality of such an act. Of course, such a policy increased the bitterness of the Radical opposition and the excitement in the country. The Liberal Government committed so many illegalities during the electoral campaign that they did not mind committing a few more. They succeeded in creating for themselves an artificial although a small and unreliable majority in the Assembly, and determined to continue their policy of intimidation and almost of terrorisation.

The political situation was undoubtedly very strained, and nobody knew how matters would end. Then something happened that nobody could have foreseen. The silent, pale, and cold-looking boy King invited the Regents and the principal Members of the Cabinet to dine with him in the Palace on the night of the 12th April. They came, and seemingly enjoyed the typically Servian dishes, for the Regency thought it their patriotic duty to accustom the young King to be patriotic even in his culinary tastes, and they consequently banished from the Palace the French chef of King Milan's celebrated French cuisine. Mr. Ristich was, as usual, grave and reserved, but his colleague the second Regent, General Belimarkovich, was more than usually gay and talkative. The Home Minister, Mr. Ribaratz, was very confident that he would be able to lead the Skupshtina successfully through its indispensable legislative work, and then adjourn it. Some witticisms were cracked at the expense of the Radical Party. The company laughed heartily. The young boy King did not join in the laugh, but he hardly ever did laugh.

The dinner was not yet ended for some reason or other the service seemed very slow, and the young King looked at his watch. He, generally so remarkably self-possessed for a boy, seemed to be somewhat distracted and restless, to such an extent as to be noticed by the members of the Government.

Then Lieutenant-Colonel Tyirich, the King's first Aide-de-Camp, entered the Banqueting Hall, walked straight up to the young King, and with a deep bow whispered something to him.

The young King rose. The company looked at him with some surprise, as it was too late to propose toasts.

"Gentlemen!" began Alexander Obrenovich, who at that very moment ceased to be a boy, and became a King, his voice not betraying the slightest nervousness or emotion.

"Gentlemen! It is announced to all the garrisons in Servia, to all the authorities, and to the people, and I announce it here to you, that I declare myself of full age, and that I now take the government of the country into my own hands. I thank you, my Regents, for your services, of which I now relieve you. I thank you also, gentlemen of the Cabinet, for your services, of which you are relieved too. You will not be allowed to leave this Palace to-night; you can remain here as my guests, but if not, then as my prisoners!"

For a few moments there was a dead silence. The Regents and the Ministers were dumbfounded. The first Regent, trembling, and with a white face, in a low and sorrowful voice said, "If it is not your Majesty's wish to allow us to exercise our mission for the legal and constitutional term, which means hardly more than a year longer, you might have appealed to our well-known loyalty to the dynasty."

General Belimarkovich reproached the King in words not so well chosen, declared his action illegal, and protested violently against it; rushed from the Banqueting Hall as if to leave the Palace. Lieutenant-Colonel Tyirich stopped him with his sword drawn, and, opening the doors, showed him in the adjoining room a company of soldiers with glittering bayonets on their rifles.

"I leave you in charge of Lieutenant-Colonel Tyirich, whose orders you will have implicitly to obey, while I go to take the oath of fidelity from the Army," said the King, and left the Hall.

Next morning (the 1st of April according to the Old Calendar, 13th of the New) the citizens were early awakened by military music playing through the streets, and the cannons firing from the fortress. They saw the walls of their town placarded with the Royal Proclamation, that King Alexander, watching with alarm the illegal actions of the Liberal Government, and fearing that if the present struggle was allowed to continue the country would drift into civil war, thought it his duty to proclaim himself of age, and had taken the reins of the Government into his own hands. Half an hour later every house unfurled the national flags, and thousands of citizens flocked in front of the Palace to cheer the young King most enthusiastically. The official *Gazette* published his first decree, forming a Radical Cabinet, under the Premiership of his principal tutor and physician, Dr. Lazar Dokich.

The majority of the Servian people were delighted by the action of the young King. The Regency was not popular, and the high-handed policy of the Liberal Cabinet during the elections and since the meeting of the Skupshtina was condemned by every impartial man in the country. The public opinion of Europe was struck by the originality of the idea and its successful execution.

The Radicals, unexpectedly receiving the government of the country into their hands, were naturally most enthusiastic about the young King. He was to them, there and then, nothing less than "Alexander the Great," according to their newspapers. Inasmuch as he stopped the somewhat fierce persecution of the Radicals by the Liberal Government, Alexander was to them "the God-sent Saviour of the country." By their exaggerated adulation and flatteries, the Radicals were the first men in Servia who encouraged the natural inclination of the King to form an exaggerated idea of his own importance, as well as to lean towards autocracy. On the very day of his taking the Government in his hands, the Radicals, probably unintentionally, and in the intoxication of their unexpected triumph secured by him for them, began to work at his demoralisation and ruin.

I was sincerely devoted to the dynasty, and was deeply saddened and alarmed by this first public and political act of my young King. It was no doubt cleverly and energetically executed; it showed a remarkable astuteness and impatience to reign, and, as it seemed to me, an immoderate ambition. I thought it not only illegal, but immoral. If King Alexander, in his seventeenth year, is capable of transforming his hospitable table into a trap, and make his guests his prisoners; if as a young man he is not guided by highest motives and principles, what can we expect of him in later years, when the struggle of life had destroyed the idealism of youth? I did not write to King Alexander, but I did write to his father, King Milan, and to some intimate friends, telling them that such an act does not foreshadow any good either for Servia or for the young King. One of those letters was published in 1894 by an enemy of mine, who wished to compromise me in the eyes of King Alexander. The King only expressed to me his astonishment that I should take such a view of his action, which he said "was even by my enemies the Radicals highly approved." "Exactly," I remarked; "just because your enemies approved of it, I cannot as your friend."

Many people suspected King Milan to be the originator of this first *coup d'état* of King Alexander. I am sure that King Milan was totally ignorant of the plan. It is evident that by the success of the intrigue, the Regents, King Milan's devoted friends, and the Liberals, the dynastic party par excellence, were defeated, and his own son and the government of the country were placed in the hands of well-known old enemies of King Milan. The plan was hatched in the head of King Alexander's tutor, Dr. Dokich, accepted eagerly by his pupil, and executed promptly by him and his first Aide-de-Camp, Tyirich, supported ably by another Aide-de-camp Major Alexander Mashin.

CHAPTER VI

KING ALEXANDER'S SECOND *COUP D'ÉTAT*

I am not writing a detailed history of political events in the Kingdom of Servia. It is my desire to give my readers insight into those great lines of political movement in that unhappy country, by which historical destiny prepared the tragical end of King Alexander and the Obrenovich Dynasty.

Servia had a young King, who had just given a startling proof of great initiative and energy, who seemed to possess considerable personal gifts of intelligence, and remarkable self-control. He was educated by a Radical politician, and was believed and expected to act as a Radical. When he appeared on the scene in the first act of his tragedy, he certainly behaved as a Radical, and showed no consideration for the artificial system created with great efforts by the Liberal Party. He placed the government of the country in the hands of his Radical tutor and his political friends. I may say that he did that not only because he had full confidence in Dr. Dokich, but more especially because he was aware of the fact that the Radical Party had the greatest majority in the country.

The leaders of the Radicals Nichola Pashich, Taushanovich, Stoyan Protich, Zivkovich were excellent political organisers. They succeeded first in drawing towards them many village priests and village teachers; made them their agents, and instructed them to try to persuade as many peasants as they could to inscribe their names in the Radical Register. The village priests and teachers succeeded rapidly in that task, especially as they did not hesitate to promise the peasants the reduction of the State taxes, abolition of the standing army, abolition of the bureaucratic system, the independence and the self-government of the communes, and many other things far in advance and above the democratic, but not demagogic, programme of the Radical Party. It is no exaggeration to say that between 60 and 70 per cent, of the entire number of the peasant voters were inscribed in the Radical Register.

Most of the leaders of the Radicals were clever politicians, but not real statesmen. Those among them who were something like statesmen *could not and did not* exercise a decisive influence in the central Council of the Party, nor on the conduct of State affairs. Among the leaders of the Radicals were several well-known agents of the Pretender to the throne, Prince Peter Karageorgevich, as for instance Ranko Tayssich, Costa Taushanovich, Atza Stanoyevich, and Lyuba Zivkovich.

Called to the Government, under the young King, with confidence in them, the Radicals might have opened an era of true liberty and progress for Servia, and of contentment and peace. But they abused their numerical power in the country and their Government majority, to oppress and persecute the two remaining political parties the Liberals and the Progressives. They inaugurated their government by impeaching the Members of the last Liberal Cabinet, and by sweeping from public office all Liberals and Progressives, replacing them by their own partisans, although these lacked the necessary qualifications for employment in the public service. This naturally provoked bitterness and resentment on the part of the two now more or less persecuted political parties. In this very first year of King Alexander's reign, political passion was in full blaze all over the country.

The Liberals and the Progressives always considered as men sincerely devoted to the dynasty of Obrenovich appealed to the King for protection against the persecution which they suffered at the hands of the Radicals, who, to say the least, were never devoted friends of Obrenovich, and of whom several leaders were more than suspected of anti-dynastic proclivities. The young King counselled his Radical Government to exercise more moderation and greater justice. He himself gave a fine example of consideration for the susceptibilities of others. In his first progress through the country he visited the grave of Kara-George in the village of Topola, and laid on it a wreath with an inscription in which he gave expression to his great respect for the leader of the first Servian insurrection against the Turks. But this generous deed flattered only the partisans of Karageorgevich and encouraged their hopes, while it correspondingly weakened the partisans of the reigning dynasty.

Having made new elections, and obtained a Skupshtina without any opposition, and having appointed its own partisans to all the places of the Civil Service, dismissing even the servants and attendants of public offices suspected to belong to the Liberal or Progressive Party, and replacing them with men inscribed in the Radical Register, the Government began to show little respect even to their "Alexander the Great" of yesterday. They resented his remonstrances with them, they took every day less and less account of his wishes and of his opinions, and even told him that he could attend the Cabinet Council only when they requested him to do so. King Alexander was deeply and personally offended by what he considered the ungrateful conduct of the Radicals. The energetic young man who ventured a dangerous *coup d'état* to wrest the power from friends of the dynasty, the Liberals, to give it to his dynasty's opponents, the Radicals, was not likely to accept meekly the insignificant role assigned to him by the men to whom he had handed the government of the country.

Taking as his justification the political chaos, the bitter dissensions, and the political, passionate struggle provoked by the narrow, selfish, and grasping policy of the Radical Government under the Radical Constitution, King Alexander dismissed the Radical Cabinet and replaced it by what he called a Neutral Cabinet, composed of moderate men of the Progressive and the Liberal Party. This was not constitutional, of course. Once engaged on the path of unconstitutional proceedings, he very soon found himself in such a dilemma that he felt obliged either to abolish the Radical Constitution, or capitulate to the Radicals, who certainly never were capable of generosity, but rather of vindictiveness, and who, now indifferent in their devotion to the reigning dynasty, did not hide their ill-will towards King Alexander. As long as the "King Milan's" Constitution remained, the Radicals with their admirable organisation, would always be able to secure a majority in the Skupshtina, and impose their leaders as the King's Ministers. He had reason to fear being again in the hands of the Radicals. He thought it would be less risky for himself personally to suspend the Constitution of 1888 and replace it by the old Constitution of 1869, which, although called Liberal, was in truth very Conservative. It was not difficult for him to find the Ministers who could dare to suspend the Radical Constitution. The political men of Servia, all equally ambitious to get the power in their own hands, competed for the Royal favours, and hated each other so passionately that they could not combine among themselves to force the King to reign constitutionally. When in the opposition, they generally tried to intimidate the young King by anti-dynastic menaces, or to win his goodwill by promising to serve him faithfully when in power. Such conduct had two consequences in the development of the young man's character: he became convinced that there was no true loyalty among the Servians, and began to believe that with sugar in one hand and a whip in the other he could best succeed in subduing to his own will the wild horse of the Servian politics. In fact, Servian politicians were corrupting their own young King, and King Alexander was corrupting the Servian political parties. Politicians sinned far more against their young King than the King sinned against them. If they had been incorruptible, or if he at his first trials had found them incorruptible, he could not have succeeded. And if they wished to make of him a good constitutional King they might have succeeded, as his youth and intelligence, with a keen political sense, gave them a very good chance.

As I have mentioned, when King Alexander made his first *coup d'état* the Radicals applauded him enthusiastically. When he made his second *coup d'état*, viz. the suspension of the Constitution of 1888, and its replacement by the old Constitution of 1869, he received congratulations from all parts of the country, and numerous deputations from the towns and villages arrived in Belgrade to thank him "that he had saved the country from further anarchy." Naturally, the Liberals were now the foremost in extolling the King's wise initiative, and praising his political genius, as the Radicals did on the occasion of his first *coup d'état*.

By such conduct of the politicians of Servia, was not the young Alexander encouraged to venture eventually on a third, or even on a fourth, *coup d'état*? Had they not given him enough cause to think contemptuously of them all, and to consider that the only politically gifted and strong man in Servia was he himself, King Alexander Obrenovich?

As a child he lived in extremely sad and demoralising circumstances, not by his own fault but by the fault of his parents.

As a boy he was, so to speak, abandoned by his mother and father, surrounded by strangers, probably quite honest, but somewhat rough, and certainly not highly cultured men, and was given an education which had no moral foundations.

And now, as the reigning King, between his seventeenth and twentieth year, from the practical political life of Servia he received daily the injunction that the principles of a Machiavellian policy were the only safe rules of conduct among the politicians whose dynastic loyalty, personal devotion, and even general patriotism, was unreliable.

Poor King Alexander! Long before his murderers plotted to destroy him, all the circumstances of his childhood and of his youth conspired against him!

CHAPTER VII

RUSSIA AND SERVIA

In this painful history of the saddest tragedy in contemporary times, the chapter which I now write is the most painful to me.

I frankly accuse Russia of having planned deliberately, and accomplished mercilessly, the ruin of the Obrenovich Dynasty. And I will show that to accomplish that object the Russian official and unofficial diplomacy did not hesitate to apply methods of such intensely Asiatic Machiavellism, that the mind and morality of Western Europe can hardly realise that such actions would have been possible at the end of the nineteenth and the beginning of the twentieth century.

I regret to have to proffer such an accusation against the Slavonic, Holy Orthodox Russia. I regret it the more as I believe it is now inevitable that the Servian nation as well as the Bulgarian nation will sooner or later be merged into, and absorbed by, the great Empire of the Tzar. The majority of the Servian people, represented as they are by the Radical Party of all shades, is already now almost more Russian than Servian.

There are altogether between five and six millions of Servians in the Balkan Peninsula, two and a half millions forming the population of the independent Kingdom of Servia. The Servians belong to the great family of Slavonic nations. Ethnographically they are first cousins to the Russians, Bulgarians, Poles, Czeks, Slovaks, and Slovenians, and they are brothers to the Croats. Their language is very similar to the Russian, only it is softer, clearer, and more musical. The letters of their alphabet are mostly identical with the Russian. With the exception of about 250,000 Catholic Servians and about 350,000 Mohammedans of Bosnia, all other Servians belong to the Orthodox

Eastern Church (the so-called Greek Church). In their churches they use the Old Slavonic language, which is identical with the language used in the Russian churches. There are, therefore, undoubtedly very important and mighty links which bind the Servian people to the Russians. To the ethnographic, linguistic, and religious bonds we must add the political bonds by which Russia, not unsuccessfully, tried to bind the Servian nation to herself.

The Servians rose in 1804, by their own free impulse and by their own initiative, against the Turks. After a few prominent men had refused to be their leader they elected The Black George Petrovich (commonly known as Kara-George) for their Supreme Leader (Verhovni Vozd). Under his leadership they fought successfully, and the largest part of the present kingdom was practically free already in 1805. In 1807 the Porte, on the eve of a war with Russia, offered to grant the Servians independence and recognise Kara-George as their Prince, Vassal to the Sultan. But Russian agents came to Servia and determined Kara-George to reject the Porte's offer and join the Servian forces with the Russian in the military operations against the Turks. The Servians fought as the Russian allies for nearly five years; but when the Russians, in 1812, were forced on the eve of the French invasion to conclude hurriedly peace with Turkey in Bucharest, they sacrificed their Servian allies, stipulating only an amnesty to be granted by the Sultan.

The Turkish forces invaded Servia in 1813, and Kara-George, after nine years hard fighting to secure his country's independence, was obliged to abandon the struggle, and left Servia, taking refuge at Kishenyeff, on Russian soil.

Milosh Obrenovich, one of the subordinate Voyvodes (Generals) of Kara-George, would not leave the country. Recognised by the Turks as the Chief of the Servian Rayah, he started a new and general insurrection of the Servians against them, on the Palm Sunday of 1815, at the small church of Takovo, in the centre of Servia. Without any aid from Russia he, after several victories, entered into negotiations with the Turks, and secured for Servia its autonomy, and for himself acknowledgment as the Prince of Servia. After this important success was achieved by the Servians themselves, the Russians began again to take interest in Servian affairs. The Russian Ambassador in Constantinople, Baron Stroganoff, was undoubtedly of very great help to Prince Milosh in his endeavours to fortify, and if possible extend the privileges already obtained from the Sultan, and

Russia rendered far more important service to Servia when, dictating the peace to Turkey at Adrianople, A.D. 1829, she introduced into the Treaty articles placing the autonomy of Servia under the Protectorate of the Tzar. Servian rights and privileges were thus placed on the basis of an international treaty.

At the same time, the further progress of Servia, in a political sense, was rather handicapped by the treaty of Adrianople. The Prince of Servia was watched, not only by his Suzerain, the Sultan, but still more jealously by his Protector, the Tzar of Russia. The Russian policy concerning Servia, as well as all other Balkan countries, was to free them from the Turkish yoke, prevent the development of a spirit of independence and self-determination, and exclude every foreign influence, more especially that of the neighbouring Austria, and practically transform the Prince of Servia into a Russian Governor-General of that country. The moment the Prince of Servia showed a disposition to serve the special interests of his own country, rather than those of Russia, he was to be deprived of power, or got rid of in some other way.

Prince Milosh, the founder of the dynasty Obrenovich, offended Russia by his great and independent initiative in serving his country. He gave the Servian people the first Constitution, without asking the approval of Russia, and the Tzar's Government at once moved the Porte to protest against the Servians having a Constitution. The Sultan and Tzar ordered Milosh to withdraw that Constitution and accept one made by the Russians and the Turks. Prince Milosh obtained from the Porte, without any assistance from and even without consulting Russia, the recognition of the hereditary right of his family to the throne of Servia. This attempt to create a Servian dynasty aroused the rage of the Russians against Milosh, and principally through their action Milosh was forced to abdicate in 1839 and go into exile.

When the Servians elected Alexander, the younger son of Kara-George, to be Prince, in 1842, Russia would not acknowledge the election, because it was made without the consultation and approval of the Tzar. The election was annulled, and the Servians had to make a new election, in the presence of the Tzar's special representative, choosing, however, again the same Alexander Karageorgevich.

When Prince Alexander accepted the resolution of his Senate that Servia should remain neutral and at peace during the Crimean War, and when he showed decidedly an inclination to listen to advices from Vienna, the Russians organised conspiracies for the dethronement, afterwards against the life, of Prince Alexander. I have had in my hands the Memoirs of one of the Senators, one of the principal conspirators against Alexander's life, who tells in detail how they have been led by the Russian Consul-General, Colonel Miloshevich, to conspire against Alexander. And when, in 1858, the National Assembly pronounced the dethronement of Prince Alexander Karageorgevich, and the recall of old Milosh Obrenovich to the throne, it was by the intrigues and assistance of Russia, which cleverly utilised the dissatisfaction among the people with Prince Alexander's weak rule.

When the noblest man on the throne of Servia during the nineteenth century, Prince Michael Obrenovich III., achieved great political success in 1867 in the evacuation of the Servian fortresses by the Turkish garrisons, and when he was preparing the insurrection of Bosnia and Bulgaria, and the proclamation of their union with Servia under himself, he was suddenly, treacherously, and cruelly murdered by the partisans of the Karageorgevich Dynasty, who hoped to seize the government and proclaim Alexander Karageorgevich or his son, Peter, Prince of Servia. Everyone felt that the partisans of Karageorgevich had been encouraged to do their bloody deed by one or other great Power. There are to this day many people who suspect Russia. I have seen no proofs either for one or for the other theory. It is, however, very comprehensible that neither Austria nor Russia would have liked to see Bosnia, Servia, and Bulgaria united under one and the same crown, and especially under such a patriotic, independent, and self-respecting man as Prince Michael Obrenovich III.

Prince Milan Obrenovich IV. was politically educated by the Regent Yovan Ristich, who on the whole was himself a Slavophil. Prince Milan, from the very beginning of his reign to the time of San Stefano Treaty (1871-1878), was so sincerely devoted to Russia that he at the instigation and insistence of General Ignyatieff, the Russian Ambassador in Constantinople, declared war against Turkey, although he knew well that the Servian army, insufficiently organised and badly equipped, must lose the campaign. But when he saw that at San Stefano Russia created a great Bulgaria, giving her even the provinces inhabited by the Servians, whereas for Servia she stipulated only a rectification of the frontier; when he saw that at the Congress of Berlin Russia allowed Austria to get two great Servian provinces, Bosnia and Hertzegovina, and fought strenuously against Servia getting Pirot and

Wranya; when the Servian representative, Yovan Ristich, was by Prince Gortchakoff himself advised to go to Count Andrassy, and try to come to agreement with Austria-Hungary then Prince Milan, indignant at such conduct of Russia towards Servia and towards himself, turned his back on her, refused to follow any longer her guidance, and, in 1882, concluded a secret convention with Austria-Hungary.

That a Servian ruler should dare turn his back on Russia, refuse to follow her guidance, and even make a secret arrangement with the supposed enemy of the Slavs concerning old Servia and Macedonia, such a diabolical phenomenon could not be for a moment tolerated by Panslavonic Russia. The honest but narrow-minded Tzar Alexander III. was indignant, and gave without hesitation his approval to the Panslavonic determination to ruin and destroy Milan Obrenovich IV. From that time to his very death, 1882-1901, King Milan was in the eyes of the Panslavonic Russia an outlaw, a wild beast whom to destroy was a meritorious Christian deed!

There was an eccentric woman in Belgrade, Helene Markovich, the widow of Colonel Yephrem Markovich, a well-known partisan of the dynasty Karageorgevich and enemy of the Obrenovich, who was condemned and executed for attempting to raise a revolt in the army at the moment when it started on the second campaign against the Turks. This woman swore to revenge the death of her husband. She went to Russia, and immediately on her return tried to kill King Milan in the very Cathedral of Belgrade, by firing on him with a Russian revolver. He escaped unhurt. It is difficult to prove that the Russians had really instigated this woman to kill King Milan; but King Milan and his Government of that time had reason to believe that she was the tool of the Russian Panslavonists.

When the attempt against the life of King Milan failed, the Radicals, the faithful friends of Russia, tried in 1883 to start a revolution against the King. Shortly before, an unusually large number of the Russian sellers of Holy Pictures (Eikons) were noticed moving from town to town, and from village to village in the districts in which the revolution was attempted. But this also failed.

Then it seems that the Chief of the Russian campaign against Milan remembered, or was told, that the only fatal weapon by which an Obrenovich could be destroyed was a woman! Very soon after we had a strange spectacle. Queen Nathalie, who boasted openly that one part of her heart was always Russian, began to force King Milan to risk a public scandal in his hatred of her, and she did everything possible, openly or secretly, to compromise her own husband, the father of her only son, in the eyes of his own people, and in the eyes of the civilised world. Queen Nathalie probably was not conscious that she acted as the tool and most virulent agent of Russia's hatred of Milan; but practically she did so. At the same time the Russians organised a campaign in the Press of all European countries against the political and private conduct of Milan.

But this was not enough. While on one side encouraging the bitter and merciless struggle of Queen Nathalie against King Milan, the Russians had at the same time gained a devoted agent in the mistress of King Milan, the Levantine lady, Mme. Arthemise, the wife of his private secretary, Mr. Milan F. Christich. Many people believe that King Milan was hypnotised by her. The fact is that, while he was under the spell of her influence he hated his wife, Queen Nathalie, and that inasmuch as, later on, that influence subsided, his animosity against Queen Nathalie diminished too.

It was Mme. Arthemise who inspired Milan to divorce his wife. And it was she who suggested to him the abdication of the crown and throne. It was King Milan who told me this, praising at the same time "the admirable wisdom" of the woman, who made the suggestion of the abdication, and who brought in support of it the most convincing arguments. Of course, it is quite possible that she made that suggestion from her own initiative, hoping that King Milan, once an ex-King, would more readily marry her, and thereby legalise the position of the boy whom she had borne to him. But it was not impossible that her Russian patrons, who worked so persistently to dethrone Milan, advised her to suggest to him the abdication, easily proving to her how much it might be in her own interest.

When, in 1897, ex-King Milan returned to Servia, settled in the Palace of Belgrade to live in the company of his son, and assumed the post of Commander-in-Chief of the Servian Army, the official as well as the unofficial Russia were exasperated against him. The Russian Press and the European newspapers, inspired by the official press-bureau of the Ministry of Foreign Affairs in St. Petersburg, were simply in a fury, attributing to him all sorts of sinister and monstrous intentions, amongst which the conversion of King Alexander from a Slavophil into an Austrophil was the most trivial. They simply called upon the Servians to rise as one man in revolt, to drive away the father of their young King. To encourage such a revolt, the Russian Minister,

Jeadovsky, openly fraternised with the Radical enemies of King Milan, and ostentatiously would not greet him when they met in the streets of Belgrade, or in the circle of the European diplomatists there.

When it became clear that the attacks in the Press, Servian and foreign, did not affect in the least the determination of King Milan to remain at the side of his son, when the services which he was rendering to the Servian Army as its Commander-in-Chief only increased the fascination which his brilliant intelligence, kindliness, and generosity exercised over the Servians, then someone in Russia came to the conclusion that the only safe method to remove King Milan for ever from Servia was to kill him. My friend Dr. Vladan, the Servian Premier from October 1897 to July 1900, published a despatch of Mr. Jeadovsky (dated in the year 1898) to his Government, in which the following phrase appears: "To save Servia and to safeguard our own [Russian] interests, it is absolutely necessary to cut through this coil [personified King Milan] as soon as possible."

On the 27th of June (O.S.) 1899, a Bosnian desperado fired from a revolver on King Milan while he was driving in an open carriage from the fortress to the Palace. Both King Milan and his Aide-de-Camp were slightly wounded. The would-be assassin was arrested. In his depositions he confessed that he had been hired by a Russian in Bucharest to kill King Milan, and that he received from him 20,000 francs to do it. When the photo of the house in which lives and works Colonel N.N., the Chief of the Russian Secret Police in Bucharest, was shown to the man, he recognised it as the one in which he was received by the Russian who hired him to execute the attempt on Milan.

The attempt did not succeed, and, from the Russian point of view, it was more than a failure, because King Milan not only was not removed from Servia, but the attempt aroused genuine sympathy with him in the whole nation. Even the most Russophil Radicals, always the enemies of King Milan, condemned it. The methods of unofficial Russia were not only the hiring of a murderer, who very nearly succeeded in killing King Milan, but also the Russian publicistic agencies all over Europe stated that this attempt on King Milan was deliberately arranged by King Milan himself! Unfortunately, King Milan, King Alexander, and his Government, made at this juncture a fatal political mistake of which I will have to say something later on.

"Unofficial Russia" was still faced by the unsolved problem how to remove King Milan, the friend of Austria and the enemy of Russia, from his strong position at the Court of his son, at the head of the Servian Army as its Commander-in-Chief, and it may be said, without exaggeration, from the hearts of a large number of Servians. Revelations in the Court of Justice in Belgrade connecting Russia with the attempt on Milan's life were too fresh and too glaring for another attempt to be tried. A revolution was less than ever possible. The task seemed to be hopeless. At the Tzar's Court, and in the Russian "official" Government, some honest and sensible people had suggested that probably the best plan would be to try and make peace with Milan, and by fair means detach him from Austria, and win him for Russia. And really, a certain detente was observed in the "hatred" of King Milan at the Court and in the Government of official Russia after the failure of the attempt on his life.

But unofficial Russia, remarkably astute, terribly unscrupulous, with unlimited means, and absolutely irresponsible, would not accept defeat. One or other of her agents remembered that in the history of the Obrenovich Dynasty woman had always been fatal to them. The position was clear enough King Alexander was madly in love with his mistress, Draga Mashin; Mme. Mashin was undoubtedly in love with her young and Royal lover, and she was known to be an ambitious woman; King Milan hated her. Could this woman not be used as a wedge between the son and father, to separate them for ever?

CHAPTER VIII

RUSSIA'S RÔLE IN THE RUIN OF ALEXANDER

I do not pretend to have read the secret instructions of the Russian Government to their agents in Servia, but certain facts have been seen and noticed even by "the man in the street" of Belgrade. Their true meaning was not at once correctly understood, but subsequent events have explained them.

Russian diplomacy made the acquaintance of Draga Mashin comparatively early enough, when King Alexander spent part of the winter of 1897 at Meran (Tyrol), and was accompanied by his mistress. The Russian Minister to Bavaria, Mr. Isvolsky, came specially from Munich to Meran on some secret mission to King Alexander, and spent there several days in company of the young King and his mistress. I daresay, although I have no undoubted proof, that on that occasion Draga placed herself unreservedly at the disposal of the Russian Government, to achieve the special objects of the Russian policy in Servia.

I have already mentioned that the members of the Diplomatic Corps in Belgrade did not hesitate to attend the weekly receptions of Mme. Draga, and to invite her to their own receptions and parties. There was, therefore, nothing extraordinary that the Russian diplomats also went to see her. Yet it was certainly remarked that the Russian Military Attaché, Colonel Taube, and his wife, were on most intimate terms with Draga, and while staying in Belgrade (they had to spend some time every year in Bucharest too) were almost daily visitors at the pretty cottage of Mme. Mashin, in Crown Street, near the Palace. Mr. Neklyudoff, Secretary of the Russian Legation, doing duty as Chargé d'Affaires, was also an assiduous visitor at Mme. Mashin's, not only on her reception days, but also on other days. It was noticed that Neklyudoff often met King Alexander at the house of his mistress, and remained with them for some time. King Milan and his faithful Dr. Vladan knew this well, but thought it nothing extraordinary that Colonel Taube and Mr. Neklyudoff paid some attention to Draga Mashin, who loved rather to parade her Russophil sentiments. The cordiality of King Alexander with them both was so great that they could not for a moment suspect that perhaps a great intrigue against them was slowly preparing at his meetings with Mr. Neklyudoff in the perfumed boudoir of his mistress.

Mr. Pera Todorovich in his Memoirs (Ogledalo iv. and v. pp. 58-63), writes as follows:

"On the 19th October 1897, the day on which King Alexander arrived in Belgrade from Paris, accompanied by his father Milan, I had at the house of a prominent Radical politician a meeting with the distinguished Russian diplomatist Mr. Z.I., and had with him a conversation which lasted fully four hours. According to the Russian diplomatist the return of King Milan to Servia meant the inauguration of great and dangerous changes in the home as well as foreign policy of Servia. In the internal policy the Liberal regime will be replaced again by the regime of *Order and Work*,' which practically means 'the Court to give orders and the people to execute them.' The promised change of the Constitution will be again adjourned at least by three or four years. In the foreign policy the inaugurated agreement with Russia will be abandoned, and Servia and Austro-Hungary are again politically to embrace each other. With Austrian millions King Milan will transform Nish into a great fortified camp, into which Austro-Hungary could in the case of necessity throw 200,000 men, command the Belgrade -Salonica road, and become the master of the South-Western part of the Balkan Peninsula. This the Servians ought never to permit to be done. They must prevent the accomplishment of Milan's plans by every means, and force him to leave Servia for good. Russia would help them to do that, but in a certain form, and under certain precautions, as it is not advisable that Russia should openly meddle with the internal questions of Servia. Russia interests herself for Servia only because your country is a Slavonic and orthodox country. She wants to save you from being transformed into Germans and Catholics. That is the only reason why Russia would be prepared to help you to get rid of King Milan. Some means must be found to force him to leave the country, and never to return. In politics the women play often very important parts. Frenchmen have good reason when they say, *'Cherchez la femme'*! Such means you ought to adopt here. King Alexander being young as he is, you will easily succeed by such methods. To separate definitely the son from his father, and to force King Milan to leave Servia for ever at the bidding of his own son, such a result a woman could only achieve. You ought to find such a woman."

"Probably you have in view a proper marriage of the King?" I asked him.

"By marriage or not, all the same! King Milan thinks to obtain for his son the hand of a German Princess, and thereby to secure for him the protectorship of Emperor William. But by such a marriage the King and Servia would be drawn into the German waters and be lost for the Slavonic idea! You Servians must prevent that by all means. And the best tool for such an object is a proper woman. This is my own idea, which I have communicated already some time ago to some of my Russian and Servian friends. *Indeed it may be that by this time something in that direction has been accomplished.*"

Mr. Todorovich draws the attention to the fact that on that very day a communication was sent from the Court to his own paper, the Male Novine, announcing that the Court lady of Queen Nathalie, Mme. Draga Mashin, had been at her own request relieved of her duties on account of her bad health. Mr. Todorovich goes on to argue that after all the report may be true, that Queen Nathalie acted on the advice of her Russian friends, when she placed her pretty "Court Lady" in the path of her young son.

If such reports could be verified they would enormously intensify the tragedy of the poor young man, the last of the Obrenovichs. Would it not be intensely tragic if a woman, to harm her hated husband, caused in the end the ruin of her own beloved son?

However, not only is it impossible to verify those reports, but other facts prove that, the moment Queen Nathalie discovered the relations of her Court lady with her son, she dismissed Mme. Mashin.

But what Queen Nathalie did not do, fate did. It would have been better if the Queen had retained Draga at Biarritz, but evidently she could not. Draga was predestined to fill one of the principal parts in the great tragedy, and she had to go to Belgrade to enjoy the love of the young King Alexander, in the shadow of the Old Palace, dreaming of the throne and the crown, without a thought of what awaited her and her beloved Sasha, a few years later on, in the same Old Palace of Belgrade! And was the poor woman, consciously or unconsciously, nothing but a fascinating servant, a beautiful but helpless tool in the hands of Russia?

I again quote from Mr. Todorovich's Memoirs: —

One day in March 1900 the Prefect of the Police, Mr. Rista Bademlich, called Mr. Todorovich to his office in the Prefecture. Both men were old friends, both sincerely devoted to King Milan and to his son.

"I want you," said the Prefect to Mr. Todorovich, "to help me, with your better knowledge of the Russian language, to find out what is the true object of a Russian who arrived in our town a few days ago, and who insists on having a private audience with King Milan. You take the place at that table, and I will introduce you to him as my private secretary."

He sent for the Russian, who in less than a quarter of an hour arrived, as he was staying at the Hotel Imperial, not far from the Prefecture. The Russian was a tall and handsome man, of middle age, with a well-groomed, greyish beard, large blue and smiling eyes, well dressed, and very distinguished-looking. When the Prefect Bademlich introduced him to Mr. Todorovich as to his private secretary, the Russian looked steadily into the face of Mr. Todorovich, and then, turning to the Prefect, said in a tone which betrayed great surprise —

"What is that? Why is that? Why this mystification? Sir, this gentleman is not your secretary, he is a journalist!" And then, turning to Mr Todorovich, he said,"Peter Todorovich, do you not remember me, Stakevich-Matushkin?"

Then Mr. Todorovitch recognised an old Russian friend, whom he knew some twenty years ago in Paris, in the circle of the Russian emigrants, and whom he met lately at the celebration of Pushkin's centenary, in Petersburg. He explained to him satisfactorily the "mystification" of his acting as pseudo-secretary of the Prefect. Then they both, Mr. Bademlich and Mr. Todorovich, tried for some time unsuccessfully to find out the nature of the communication which he wished, "under four eyes," to communicate to King Milan. But he persisted in refusing it, only assuring them that King Milan would not repent if he received him, and he left them, saying that he intended to leave Belgrade at once. Mr. Todorovich followed him, and had all sorts of interesting talk with him. At the moment of taking leave of each other, Matushkin looked for some moments straight into the eyes of his Servian friend, and then said with evident emotion, and great emphasis —

"Peter Todorovich, listen! Not six months will pass from this day, and you will have here in Servia a great crisis and a fatal political change. All the plans of King Milan will be destroyed. He himself will be brutally removed from Servia. King Alexander will fall into Russian slavery, he will be married to a common woman who is in no respects a proper party for him, he will remain without children, and will be entirely ruined. Servia may be in such a position that she may, indeed, disappear as an independent State. And all this will be done by perfidious Russian policy, using as a tool a common woman, and what astonishes me as still more extraordinary a Servian woman! Peter Todorovich, remember what I have told you this day! Good-bye!"

This is the faithful abstract of the detailed statement published by Mr. Todorovich in his Memoirs, Ogledalo v. pp. 63-70.

As I did not approve of King Alexander's marriage with Mme. Draga Mashin, I was, shortly after their wedding, informed that I was to be replaced in Constantinople as Servian Minister by General Sava Grooich, a Panslavist and therefore a *persona gratissima* at the Russian Court. I wish to take this opportunity to say with grateful acknowledgment that, although I was well known not to belong to the Panslavists, I was always most generously treated and supported, during the few months of my activity in Constantinople, by the Russian Ambassador, Mr. Zinovieff.

On my way from Constantinople to Abazzia I stopped for a few days in Belgrade to pay my respects to the King, and to see the new Queen of Servia. 1 had visited many gentlemen and lady friends in the highest Belgrade society, and found the general impression prevalent that the marriage of Alexander with Draga was the work of the Russian policy. Everybody assured me that the general consternation was dispelled or rather replaced by another consternation, and the opposition of the Church, the army, and of the people at large, weakened the moment it was announced, that the Tzar was to be the "Koom" at the marriage, and that he had congratulated Alexander on his engagement with Draga.

One of the ladies belonging to the upper ten of Belgrade society, the wife of a General, who was rather an intimate friend of Draga Mashin before she became the Queen of King Alexander, told me what in her own circle of lady friends was believed to be the true story of how this fatal marriage came about.

"Of course," began Madame N.N., "we all knew that King Alexander was much in love with Draga, and that she simply adored him. How often have I not said to her: "Look here, Draga, thou beautifiest thyself too much, and there is no wonder that the King is so much in love with thee. But surely thou willst not turn his head to that degree that he might make thee the Queen of Servia?' Draga would always jump up in rage and indignation: 'What thinkest thou I am? I hate thee for talking such nonsense. Thou knowest I adore Sasha, and just because I adore him I shall never stand for a moment between him and his duty. He must marry a foreign Princess, who would bring him valuable political connections, wealth, perhaps even true happiness, and I will gladly sacrifice my own happiness to his!' We knew also that she really spoke in the same way to King Alexander.

"Then the Russian General N. N. arrived in Belgrade. You know him? Well you must know whom he married?"

"No," I said. "I knew him as a bachelor, who had a Roumanian girl for his mistress."

"Very well," continued my friend, "the very same girl became his wife. During their prolonged stay here they went often to Draga, and she became soon very fond of the General's wife. The little Roumanian told her one day that, although the General was very fond of her, he never meant to marry her, until she heard of an old Roumanian witch, somewhere in the neighbourhood of Plojesti, went to see her, and for a few napoleons obtained from her the assurance that she would make him marry her, and a charm which she gave her General to drink in a cup of coffee.

"Not quite two weeks after this assurance, and not a week after that coffee, the General one morning rose up, seemingly absorbed in deep and melancholy thoughts. 'What is the matter?' his little Roumanian sweetheart asked. 'A great deal is the matter!' answered the General, always lost in thought. 'My conscience tells me that our present relations ought not to be continued, and that, if I am an honest and honourable man, I ought to make you, before God and before men, my lawful wife.' She laughed at him, and refused him. He repeated his offer, and she repeated her refusal, every morning through a whole week, until at last the General said that he had no alternative but to marry her, and face bravely the reproaches of his relatives and friends, or to kill himself! The Roumanian sweetheart of the old General then gave her consent. Telling that story with all the details, she asked Draga to give her some of her own hair, and some of King Alexander's, and she would, on her own responsibility, see the Plojesti witch again. We, of course, do not know if Draga did really send her and the King's hair to the Plojesti witch, but we all conclude that she must have done so, seeing that King Alexander behaved exactly as the Russian General.'

I reproduce this story here, not because I think it may be perfectly true in all its details, but because it was largely believed amongst the ladies of Belgrade, and because it is a picturesque illustration of the general belief that the marriage of King Alexander with Draga Mashin was prearranged by Russia.

CHAPTER IX

MADAME DRAGA MASHIN

It is remarkable what a fatal influence woman exercised on the life and political career of the Princes of the Obrenovich Dynasty.

Prince Milosh Obrenovich I. was an exceedingly gifted and energetic man, a true-born leader of men, not only the founder of a dynasty, but the founder and the creator of the autonomous Servian Principality. A strong man in the struggle with men and political difficulties, he had a great weakness for the female sex. His infidelities gave just cause for resentment to his once very beautiful wife, Princess Lubitza, and that resentment gave a powerful assistance to the opponents of Prince Milosh. Without the domestic trouble caused by the jealousy (perfectly justified) of his wife, Prince Milosh probably would not have been sent into exile in 1839.

Prince Michael Obrenovich IV. was altogether a noble man, a great patriot, and an able statesman, the finest individuality in the history of Servia during the nineteenth century. By his diplomacy he obtained without war or other sacrifice the evacuation of the Turkish fortresses on the Servian territory. Yet his separation from his beautiful but childless wife, Princess Julia (*née* Countess Hunyady), and his intention to marry Katharina, the daughter of his cousin, Mme. Anka Constantinovich, gave to the partisans of Karageorgevich one of the pivots by which they raised up dissatisfaction amongst the people against even such a generous man and successful ruler. While he was walking with his cousin (Mme. Anka) and her daughter, accompanied only by an aide-de-camp, on a lonely path in the forest of Koshootnyak, he was, on the fatal 29th May (Old Style) 1868, attacked by conspirators and cruelly murdered.

What bitterness and humiliation, what dissatisfaction in the country and in Europe at large, was created by the unseemly and undignified quarrel between King Milan and Queen Nathalie is well known. And I have not the slightest doubt that the fatal resolve, the abdication, was instilled into his mind by his mistress, Mme. Arthemise Christich.

The terrible end of King Alexander Obrenovich V. was mainly brought about, and the tragedy of his life deepened, by his love for Draga Mashin.

One of the more prominent and influential Servians who supported Milosh Obrenovich, when he invited the people to rise again against the Turks (Palm Sunday, 1815, at Takovo Church), was Nikola Lunyevitza. It is not clear if ever he commanded a body of armed Servians in the insurrection against the Turks, or if he ever had been called a Voyvode; but there is no doubt that he was a man of good common sense, calm and wise judgment, and as a successful exporter of cattle and pigs from Serviahad made lots of money. He was patriotic enough to lend Milosh Obrenovich money whenever he wanted to buy arms. Milosh liked him, and esteemed him so much that he made him his "pobratim" — "adopted brother." Milosh Obrenovich and Nikola Lunyevitza never addressed each other otherwise than as "Pobratime," namely, "Thou who art as a brother to me."

The son of this Nikola Lunyevitza, Panta, was Prefect of Shabatz during the earlier years of King Milan's reign. Towards the end of his life he became unhinged in his mind, and died in an asylum. He had several daughters, of whom the second bore the very popular name "Draga," which, in the Servian language, means "The dear one."

This "dear one" was a very pretty girl, with elegant figure, pale, yet peculiarly warm complexion, finely cut features, and with wonderfully beautiful, velvety-brown, large and very expressive eyes. When quite a schoolgirl she married Svetozar, the youngest son of Dr. Mashin, a Czek (Bohemian) by birth, but a naturalised Servian citizen, a successful and skilful doctor, but rather unpopular on account of his bad temper and unscrupulous principles.

Svetozar Mashin was a mining engineer by profession, in the employment of the Ministry of Finance. He died after hardly a year of his wedded life, somewhat suddenly, but not mysteriously. The enemies of Queen Draga liked to spread the report that she had poisoned her first husband. But at the time of his death I was Minister of Finance, and he one of my secretaries of the Mining Department, and as such was ordered to manage for a short time one of the Government's mining establishments. I remember at the time I was told that my secretary died of delirium tremens, and I was not surprised, as I knew him to be a hard drinker.

A young and pretty widow, with a very small fortune, and still smaller pension (which, I think, was not more than £3 per month, which she drew from the Government as the widow of a State employé), she was surrounded by many admirers, dangers, and temptations. Queen Nathalie, who delighted in doing good and charitable actions, was told that this pretty and bright young woman was a granddaughter of Prince Milosh's "Pobratim," and she took at once very deep interest in her. I am sure the Queen would not have done that if she knew that the rumours already set in motion about her love intrigues with gentlemen had any real foundation. Noticing that her education was only that which a daughter of the middle-class people could enjoy in Servia, the Queen paid teachers of foreign languages for her, and inspired in her the taste for reading French and German books. She made remarkable progress, and her Royal benefactress was quite proud to introduce such a pretty, witty, and apparently cultured young Servian lady to the families of the foreign diplomatists accredited to the Servian Court.

She moved in the very best society in the Servian capital, and was received everywhere with much pleasure. Of course, in a small town like Belgrade, tongues are sharper than in a great town, and imagination tries always to supply the *Chronique Scandaleuse* with invented stories, for want of real facts. Many an envious Belgrade beauty had only one explanation for the pretty young widow's frequent visits to the Palace, namely, that she was the mistress of King Milan! The intimate friends of King Milan knew well who his mistress was, or, to be more precise, who his mistresses were, since 1880, at different periods. I can safely say that Draga Mashin never was the mistress of King Milan. A great "psychic" as he was, he had from the very beginning of her connection with the Court a sort of aversion for her. At the time I used to explain that aversion by the fact that Draga Mashin was one of the favourites of Queen Nathalie, and King Milan could not bear the favourites of his wife.

When Queen Nathalie in 1890 decided to settle in France, and built for herself a pretty villa, "Sashino," at Biarritz, she took Draga Mashin as her *Dame d'honneur*. To be permanently in the company of such a woman as Queen Nathalie was really a liberal education in itself. As the Queen's company was constantly sought by the best and highest French, Spanish, and Russian nobility, and as during the Biarritz season many distinguished English and American families visited the Queen at "Sashino," Madame Draga Mashin had extraordinary opportunities of making acquaintance with the very best society in Europe. She was much admired, and made many friends. After she became Queen of Servia I have on one occasion seen in her boudoir at the Old Palace in Belgrade, hundreds of photographs of most distinguished ladies and gentlemen, whom she made her friends at Biarritz as Queen Nathalie's *Dame d'honneur*.

It is only fair to say that the accusations, which, after her marriage with King Alexander, her personal enemies, and the enemies of the Obrenovich Dynasty, threw out against her, as if she had been a woman of loose character, seem to me to be without foundation. I, personally, do not know a single fact which could be construed in that sense against her, except the fact that she became the mistress of King Alexander. I admit that my testimony is not worth much, as I did not watch her career. But I am sure that a woman so absolutely virtuous as Queen Nathalie, and at the same time a woman so wide-awake, so sharp, so decisive and uncompromising, and one who had extraordinary means to know and to hear, would not have taken Draga Mashin as her *Dame d'honneur* if she had the slightest cause of suspicion as to her character. The very fact that Queen Nathalie took Draga to her Court in 1890 speaks in favour of Draga's character up to that time.

Nor is it likely that while she was living in Sashino, permanently under the eyes of Queen Nathalie, she could have indulged in love intrigues with anyone. The moment Queen Nathalie possessed one of her letters, proving that she had a love intrigue with King Alexander, she dismissed her at once. As a young, pretty, and spirited woman, surrounded by flattering and admiring, perhaps even adoring, men, young and old, she might have indulged in some flirtation, but in my opinion, and to my best knowledge, she was the mistress of only one man - King Alexander.

There is a curious incident belonging to the time Draga Mashin was Queen Nathalie's Court lady. The story was told confidentially to some intimate friends by Mademoiselle Tzana Gyorgyevich, who acted for some time at Biarritz as Queen Nathalie's Maid of Honour (*Demoiselle d'honneur*), while Draga functioned as Lady of Honour.

One day (I do not know exactly what year, between 1890 and 1897) the Queen went to Paris to visit her sister, Princess Ghica, and took both her ladies with her. Before returning from Paris she went, accompanied by Madame Draga and Mademoiselle Tzana, to see and consult the famous Parisian clairvoyante, Madame Thebes. What she told the Queen is not reported, except that she said: "Your Majesty is cherishing in your bosom a poisonous snake, which one day will give you a mortal wound." To Mademoiselle Tzana she said that she would never marry (and she is still unmarried when I write this!). To Madame Draga Mashin she said: "You have great ambition, you will have an extraordinary career, you will marry the highest personage in the country; but you will bring only ruin to your husband, and you will perish with him."

After the marriage of King Alexander with Draga Mashin, this extraordinary story appeared in one of the Servian newspapers, and naturally created a great sensation. Both Queen Draga and King Alexander were exceedingly annoyed, and as Draga suspected Mademoiselle Tzana of having communicated it to the Press, poor Mademoiselle Tzana was summoned before the Prefect of the Police, to show why she should not be punished for an indiscretion, which was disturbing the peace of the Royal couple, as well as of the loyal citizens. Mademoiselle Tzana requested and obtained permission to see the Queen, and proved to her that she was innocent.

King Alexander seems to have been in certain respects abnormally constituted. The question is rather a physiological one, and of a delicate nature. On one occasion a doctor, who knew the young King very well, told me that he doubted if King Alexander would ever have an heir to the throne. In 1895 King Milan told me in Paris that, although his Sasha was quite a brilliant *garçon*, in one point he astonished him; not only that in the society of ladies he is absolutely gauche, but that he seemed to be absolutely impervious to the influence of the most charming women in the world! Poor King Milan did not know at that time that there was someone in the world, and not very far from Paris, a woman to whose charms his brilliant, but otherwise cold, son had already succumbed.

King Alexander informed me on one occasion (after his marriage) that he fell in love with Draga whilst visiting his mother, Queen Nathalie, at Biarritz, in 1897. He said the same thing to Mr. Vukashin Petrovich, the temporary President of his Government in 1900. For a month or six weeks he was constantly in the company of the fascinating young widow, not always under the vigilant eyes of his mother. He and Draga went almost daily for a ride on their bicycles, and often quite alone. They used to swim in the sea together, or rather to take lessons in swimming together. Many people blame Queen Nathalie for allowing her son to be so much, and in such risky circumstances, with her attractive *Dame d'honneur*, and some even suspected that she intentionally led him to fall in love with her "Court Lady," in order to displace altogether King Milan's influence with his son. Certainly neither Milan nor Nathalie, in their hatred of each other, were over scrupulous in selecting their weapons; but whoever knew Queen Nathalie's character, would also know that she was incapable of such a mean and dangerous intrigue. She wanted, naturally, to see her "Sasha" pleased and happy, and she had full confidence in her *Dame d'honneur*.

King Alexander told the Minister, Vukashin Petrovich, that Draga, when he fell in love with her, was an absolutely virtuous woman, that she rejected with indignation his advances, that on one occasion, when in blind passion he entered her room in the Villa Sashino, she peremptorily asked him to leave at once, and when he hesitated she took him by the shoulders, pushed him out, and turned the key in the door. Of course, such conduct added fresh fuel to the fire of his love. But was the conduct of the young widow the conduct of an honourable woman, or was it but the clever acting of a schemer? If the poor boy took it as the honourable conduct of an honest woman, and his virtuous and experienced mother thought her Court lady perfectly honest and reliable, what right have we to declare that Draga Mashin acted only as a clever but unscrupulous, designing woman?

King Alexander told the same Minister, Vukashin Petrovich, that Draga resisted his advances for more than three years. But they seem to have been writing to each other endearing love-letters. One of these fell into the hands of Queen Nathalie. She was dumbfounded by the discovery. In a great rage she ordered her Court lady, and for years her favourite, to leave Sashino for ever. Not satisfied with this, Queen Nathalie wrote to some of her lady friends that Draga Mashin had betrayed 'her confidence, and behaved as a "bad woman."

Draga Mashin left Sashino, and came to Belgrade, to become the mistress of King Alexander.

A small, but pretty and comfortable, house was engaged in the neighbourhood of the Old Palace, sumptuously furnished, and Draga Mashin installed as its mistress.

King Milan hated the woman, but thought himself not justified in interfering in the love-affair of "his King and master" as he loved to call his son. Dr. Vladan Georgevich, the Premier, as he tells us himself in his remarkable Memoirs, tried even once in the discussion with the Prefect of the Belgrade Police to justify his King and master for having this one and only mistress. The Archbishop Inokentiye knew of it, and never opened his lips to say a word on the immorality of such relations. All the officers, all the citizens, knew about it; all the diplomatists, and even the most distinguished among them went to the weekly receptions of Madame Draga, and invited her to their dinners and entertainments.

CHAPTER X

THE REGIME OF "WORK AND ORDER"

In September 1897 I asked and at once obtained permission to come for a day or two from London to Paris, to pay my respects to King Alexander, who had arrived there on his return to Servia from Biarritz, where he had been staying for some time, and for the last time, with his mother, Queen Nathalie.

Both King Alexander and his father, King Milan, received me most graciously, and retained me as their guest ten days, until their own departure for Servia.

The King confided to me that he was going to take his father with him to Servia, and keep him there at his side permanently, in spite of the "shameful" law which the Radicals, "the enemies of the dynasty," passed during his minority, forbidding the return of King Milan to Servia. Further, he told me that his intention was, immediately on his return to Belgrade, to dismiss the Radical Cabinet of George Simich, and replace it by a non-partisan Cabinet under Dr. Vladan Georgevich. He hoped Dr. Vladan, whom he had ordered to meet him in Vienna, would accept the mission; but if he should not do so, then, the King said, "With all my knowledge of the weaknesses of your Puritanic heart, and of your intolerable Quakerism, I shall have no other choice but to appeal to you!" Both King Milan and King Alexander thought that many of my notions were those of a Puritan, or even of a Quaker, and often called me the latter as a nickname.

Now I thought that policy altogether a mistaken one. I knew to what a waste of national energy led the political struggle between King Milan and the Radicals, numerically the most powerful party in Servia. I thought, further, that in the interests of the dynasty, as well as of the country, it was advisable to let the Radicals govern the country, to learn to be a party capable of governing, which means a party of moderation. Office, in my opinion, was the only school in which the better elements among the Radical politicians would learn to be true statesmen. The holding of office would make many *bonâ fide* Radicals friends of the dynasty, would weaken and divide those who are her enemies. Besides, I knew personally several members of the Radical Cabinet of that time, as, for instance, Mr. George S. Simich, and Mr. Michael Vouich, to be highly cultured and honourable men. Of course, I knew well also that Dr. Vladan, my schoolfellow and friend from our earliest schooldays, was one of the ablest and the most energetic statesmen whom we had, a first-rate orator and organiser; but in spite of all I advised the King strongly not to separate himself from his Radical Cabinet, and to continue to try and conciliate all the moderate elements of the Radical Party.

King Alexander explained to me that he had special dynastic reasons, besides general political reasons, why he had decided to form a non-partisan Cabinet, composed of men in whom he could absolutely trust.

"You know," said King Alexander to me, "that by political education I am a Radical, as much as my father, by his personal way of thinking, was a Progressive. You know that I have twice delivered myself into the hands of the Radicals, and each time they themselves gave me unmistakable proofs that I ought not to trust them. You are right when you say that George Simich and Michael Vouich are highly cultured men, and the most moderate politicians among the Radicals. But even these best of Radicals, into whose hands I have placed the country, how do they behave towards me and the dynasty? Their political chief and their Minister in Russia, Mr. Pashich, entered into negotiations with Russia to replace me on the throne of Servia by a Russian Grand Duke!

"You are astonished? . . . But there is no doubt about it. My father and myself have had proofs in our hands. But hear this story —

"Simich and Vouich take me to Cettinje, under the pretext of returning the visit Prince Nicholas made me last year. Once there, they startle me by saying I cannot decently leave Cettinje without being engaged to the Prince's daughter Xenia! I told them in the first place they ought to have told me that before we started on our journey. Besides, I informed them on several occasions since they became my Ministers that I would marry only the woman whom I found attractive, with whom I was in love, and Princess Xenia, notwithstanding her many charms, had not made me fall in love with her. Then, how did they behave in another matter? I authorised them to negotiate with Prince Nicholas for a secret treaty of alliance concerning our common interests in Old Servia and Macedonia. They agreed, without asking me, and without hesitation, that the most important towns in Old Servia, among others Prizren, the old capital of the Servian Empire, should belong not to the King of Servia but to the Prince of Montenegro. Of course, I refused to give my sanction to such a stipulation, but this refusal put me in an awkward position with the Prince. Now, how can you expect me to trust them any longer? Yes, let me show you by another example how my Radical Ministers behave towards me. On my arrival from Biarritz I was received at the station by the staff of our Paris Legation, many Servian students, and Colonel Vlaich. 'What has brought you here, Colonel?' I asked, thinking that he was there perhaps on some private business. 'I am, Sire, here on a special official mission, to negotiate with the French Government for the purchase of rifles for our army,' answered Vlaich. 'Indeed!' I said; 'and I never heard a word about it!' 'I am astonished to learn that your Majesty has not been asked to approve of this mission,' added the Colonel, evidently disconcerted. 'So am *I* astonished,' I answered. And now, what do you say to that, my dear defender of the Radicals?"

In King Alexander's suite were Colonel Laza Petrovich, Lieutenant-Colonel Milivoy Nicolayevich, and Dr. Milichevich, the King's private secretary. Both officers did not hesitate to tell the King, on several occasions, when we discussed the impending change, that they were of my opinion. Dr. Milichevich, the most discreet of men, did not express his opinion in the presence of the King; but I knew that he, too, shared my views and my arguments.

King Milan confirmed what King Alexander told me about Mr. Pashich's secret negotiations with Russia, for placing a Russian Grand Duke on the throne of Servia. He added that unmistakable proofs had been obtained and placed before him and his son, by the intervention of a friendly Power. "The Russian intrigue to get Servia into her power is so persistent, great, and dangerous, that I consider it my duty to return to Belgrade, to be at the post of danger, and to help this poor and friendless young man to preserve his throne."

I think this is the first time the true motives for the return of King Milan to Servia, and for King Alexander's change of home and foreign policy, have been published. I have no other proof, except my own word of honour, that both Kings Alexander and Milan informed me of those motives, as I have shown. The bitter and persistently inimical attitude of Russia against the new regime in Servia, proves indirectly the truth.

King Alexander explained to me that there were some other reasons why he was convinced that it was his patriotic duty to change the home policy. He did not wish to abolish the constitutional regime, but he had now enough experience with that regime to be justified in saying that Party Government, in a country with such a passionate, insufficiently educated, intolerant, and economically poor people, is far from being a blessing; it was rather a curse than a blessing. He adopted his father's idea that an immense majority of the Servians of our time had only municipal and provincial horizons, and that their political education had not as yet risen so high as to be able to take a larger view of State interests. That was the reason why, in the political life of Servia, since we had something like a parliamentary regime, State interests very often were sacrificed to petty municipal or provincial considerations. He wanted to try a new political experiment, form and keep a Liberal Government, which would be equally just to all parties and to all interests, preserve order, stimulate discipline, and encourage productive work in all spheres of public activity, cultural as well as economical.

In Vienna, he met Dr. Vladan, and, together with his father, insisted on his acceptance of the Premiership in the new Cabinet. As the programme which Dr. Vladan developed agreed in all its essential points with the ideas of the King, the matter was satisfactorily settled. On October 11th (23rd), 1897, the official Gazette published the Royal decrees appointing Dr. Vladan Georgevich President of the Council of Ministers, and Minister for Foreign Affairs. But on that very day a sign of Dr. Vladan's weakness, and of King Alexander's unconstitutionalism, was given. Dr. Vladan wrote the programme of his Government. But instead of being published as such, namely, as the programme of Government, King Alexander took it as his own programme, the execution of which he expected from Dr. Vladan's Cabinet. Putting, however, aside that formal discrepancy with the constitutional theory, the autograph letter, addressed by King Alexander to Dr. Vladan, is one of the best proofs that the young King was gifted with great political ability and true statesmanship.

I give its full text here —

"MY DEAR MR. VLADAN GEORGEVICH, — The events which have happened lately in the East, and the unmistakable determination of Europe to keep the general peace, have created for Servia the possibility and the duty to strengthen herself financially, economically, as well as her military position. This period of assured peace in Europe ought to be utilised by Servia to end the fruitless political struggle among parties, in which our country has lost so much precious time, which otherwise could have been used for political and national progress. We ought to take advantage of this period of peace to secure for our country order and lawfulness, by a conscientious, and, for all and everyone, impartial administration. By an irreproachable justice, we must prove that the law is always the most exalted power in Servia. To that we ought to add the most scrupulous performance of all the engagements of our Government, a new law concerning the State Service, and such a reform of our national education that young men who finish the schools must not look exclusively to the State Service to gain a livelihood.

"Through earnest work in the consolidation of Servia, we will be able to make of our country a healthy, progressive State, a safe and strong support for the order and peace in the Balkan Peninsula, a State on which Europe, in her pursuit of high objects of civilisation, could rely. Acting in this way, we will gain for Servia the friendship of all the European Powers, and strengthen further the friendships which we have already won. At the same time we would then prove to the world that without Servia's consent nothing could be decided affecting her interests.

"Such work will contribute materially to quiet down political passions. To attain this object is absolutely necessary, because otherwise the question of a new Constitution could not be solved naturally, but only partially, which would be dangerous for the vital interests of the people.

"'*Servia above everything else.*' A strong, and by the world a well-respected Servia was the ideal of my predecessors; it is also one to which I will consecrate my life.

"To be able to work more successfully at this, my life-task, I address myself to your proven patriotism, and your fidelity to the throne, and confide to you the difficult but honourable mission to form a new Government, which shares my above-explained convictions. The object which my new Government will have to accomplish is so difficult, that no human power could attain it, without the necessary time, and without the assurance of the stability in the work of the State. I assure my new Government of that stability, and of the period necessary for the desired success."

Dr. Vladan himself, as I have said, a man of high culture, great abilities, and the most remarkable energy had in his Cabinet many members of experience and acknowledged abilities. Without delay they began to work at the reorganisation of the national finances, production, and education. And although they had to contend with immense difficulties, thrown in their path by Russia, they obtained very considerable success.

King Milan, appointed Commander-in-Chief of the Army, took in hand the reorganisation of the Servian military forces. All the foreign military attachés were unanimous in praising the progress which the Servian Army, under his guidance, made in two years. He gained great popularity among the officers. If he had chosen he might any day, without the slightest difficulty, have superseded his son on the throne. But he rejoiced to give an example of devotion and loyalty to the young King. He never mentioned his son without saying, "My exalted son, His Majesty the King." He liked to show publicly on every occasion his great respect for him. He and Dr. Vladan thought they were working to strengthen the monarchical principle among the people. They succeeded in that object but partially, and at the same time they only aroused in the young King an exaggerated idea of his own importance and power. Instead of working together to inspire him with the desire to act as a constitutional King, and to educate him for such a position, they probably unintentionally deepened and developed in him autocratic tendencies. Especially my friend Dr. Vladan sinned terribly in that respect. Poor fellow, no one suffered more later on from the results of the political education which he, during his regime of "Work and Order," gave to that already demoralised *enfant terrible* on the throne. I always thought that a practice, introduced by Dr. Vladan, must have especially deplorable consequences, namely, when the Government had any difficulty in passing their measures before the legislative body, Dr. Vladan would ask the King to call the most prominent members of the Skupshtina not rarely the entire Skupshtina to the Palace, and to ask them to sacrifice their personal convictions and vote the Government measures to please him. Both the King and the Skupshtina were demoralised by such proceedings. The young King, always successful whenever he wished to have his own way with his Government and with the Skupshtina, concluded that there was nothing he could not get from them if he only insisted on it. The Skupshtina, yielding so often to the "charming pressure" (*douce violence*) of the eloquent young King, and, invited so frequently to sacrifice itself in the service of "the Monarchical Principle," lost its independence, the respect which it enjoyed before in the country, and even its own self-respect.

On the other hand, it must be acknowledged that the complete harmony between the King, his Government, and the Skupshtina, really established perfect order in the country, and enabled it to make considerable progress in almost every direction of public life.

This happy state of things did not last long.

Its first rude interruption was by the so-called "*St. John's Day's Attempt*" on the life of King Milan (June 24th (July 6th) 1899), and its end by the marriage of King Alexander with Mme. Draga Mashin.

I have previously stated what were the relations between Russia and Servia during the nineteenth century. I have to add here a few particulars relating especially to the regime of "Work and Order."

In the beginning of the year 1897, an important political arrangement was made between Russia and Austro-Hungary concerning the Balkan Peninsula. The text of that arrangement has never been published, and therefore, outside the Russian and Austro-Hungarian Ministers who made it, nobody knows positively its stipulations. However, in diplomatic circles the general impression was that there were only two stipulations: one to keep up the status quo in the Balkans; and the other one, that neither Austro-Hungary nor Russia should interfere with the internal affairs of the Balkan States.

The return of King Milan to Servia seriously alarmed not only the Panslavonic, but also Official Russia. Non-official Panslavonic Russia feared that Milan, the personification of anti-Panslavonism, would try naturally to displace Panslavonic ideals by exclusively Servian ideals instead of preparing the Servians for a union with Russia he would concentrate their energy to the realisation of what he called "the Servian idea," namely, the formation of a great, strong, and really independent Servian Empire. Official Russia knew that the sympathies of King Milan were with Austro-Hungary, and his antipathies with Russia. They feared that he would be the willing tool of Austro-Hungary, her willing agent in everything that could disturb Russian policy in the Balkans. Indeed, Official Russia suspected for some time that it was Austro-Hungary who brought about the return of King Milan to Servia. I was told that the Russian Foreign Minister remonstrated in a friendly spirit with Count Goluchowsky, and wanted the Austro-Hungarian Government to use its reputed influence with

King Milan to leave Servia, otherwise his sojourn in Servia would practically mean the preponderance of the Austro-Hungarian influence there, which would be contrary to the spirit of their arrangement. Count Goluchowsky denied that Austro-Hungary had anything to do with the return of King Milan to Servia, and that her eventual attempt to persuade him to leave the country would just constitute the interference in the internal affairs of an independent Balkan Kingdom which they both promised not to do.

Austrian co-operation for the amicable removal of Milan from Servia having been denied her, Russia immediately organised the campaign against Milan. As King Alexander and the Government of "Work and Order" stuck faithfully to King Milan, as indeed the new régime of Dr. Vladan had been established on the supposition that King Milan remained in the country, and at the head of the army, the Russian campaign was directed, not only against King Milan, but against King Alexander and his Government too.

In every important capital of Europe, the Russians had organised special bureaus, whose exclusive task was to spread and publish in the papers all sorts of disparaging statements about Milan. Such a bureau was established in London, too, at the head of which a Frenchman, decorated with a high Russian Order, was placed, having a Polish Jew journalist, who wrote English well, as his assistant. Secret agents, male and female, all over the world, had got orders to malign King Milan on every occasion. I knew personally of a Russian Princess who used to give luncheon and dinner parties at the sumptuous and costly Claridge's Hotel, entertaining her English guests with all sorts of stories some perhaps true, but many that I heard her tell certainly invented about the Russian *bête noire*, Milan of Servia.

In Servia the "Asiatic Department," to which the Russian management of Milan and his country belonged, did not need special agents. The Radicals of Servia, always intensely Russophil, many of them personally devoted to the Pretender, most of them opposed to Milan for his "Austrophilism," were only too eager to serve Russia. Through them the agitation in Servia against Milan, and, indeed, against the Obrenovich Dynasty, was organised and nourished. But the cause of the dynasty of "Order and Work" was defended by three men probably the ablest in all Servia, namely, Milan, Alexander, and Dr. Vladan, who, moreover, had the army and the State power in their hands. No wonder that the agitation, started and organised by the Russians, and carried on in Servia by the partisans of Peter

Karageorgevich and by the *bona fide* Russophil Radicals, did not succeed in the least. The advantages of order had been soon felt in the increased prosperity throughout the country. The great mass of the peasantry did not conceal its satisfaction. Even the Eastern districts (Krayina, Zaechar, Knyazevatz), which of old were always Radical Russophil and pro-Karageorgevich, received King Alexander and his father in 1899 with great cordiality and loyalty.

One of the reasons why the anti-dynastic agitation had no success was in the old methods of the Russian and Radical tactics. They spread again lies and calumnies, which they had used during the last eighteen years, and of the falseness of which the people of Servia had ample time to assure themselves. They again asserted that King Milan had sold Servia to Austria for hard cash, that he was eating up the millions collected from the people in taxes and other public imports, using them to pay off his immense debts, contracted in Paris in gambling, and in keeping his mistresses in a sumptuous style; that he had returned to Servia to fulfil his engagement towards the Roman Catholic Pope to turn the Servians from orthodoxy, and convert them by force into Roman Catholics; that he had concluded a Military Convention with Austria, with the object of destroying the power of Russia, that he might afterwards, when Russia was no longer in a position to protect Servia, place his country under Austrian rule. The only new variation in these old and exploded calumnies was: That Milan's programme was to get first the army under his control (which had been already accomplished), marry his mistress, Arthemise, the divorced wife of his former private secretary, Milan Christich, legalise the position of the illegitimate boy whom he had by Arthemise, then put his own son King Alexander into an asylum, or eventually poison him, ascend the throne for the second time, and declare Arthemise's son the heir-presumptive. This version made some impression, because it looked so plausible, although it had not the slightest foundation in fact.

Another reason for the want of success was in the altogether mistaken notion of the Russian Government on the true situation in Servia. The reports of their agents regarding the alleged dissatisfaction in Servia were too exaggerated. According to them, nothing was needed but a visible proof that the Almighty Tzar of all the Russias was against the Obrenovich and for Karageorgevich, and the people would rise at once, drive away Alexander and Milan, and recall Karageorgevich. The Tzar made one of those demonstrations by placing most graciously the young sons of Prince Peter Karageorgevich in the officers' school for nobility in St. Petersburg. Before that, Mr. Jeadovsky was sent as the Russian Minister to Belgrade on a special mission, to show the people of Servia that the Tzar did not care for the Obrenovich Dynasty, that he hated and despised Milan, and that he would not take any interest in the welfare of Servia so long as Milan remained in that unhappy country. Jeadovsky did not hesitate to denounce and calumniate King Milan to every Servian politician or citizen with whom he came in contact, calling him the most opprobrious names. He went even so far as to insult King Milan, taking no notice of him when they met in society, and refusing to salute him in the streets of Belgrade. He expected that such conduct would prove to the Servians that Milan was a man of no consequence to Russia, that he was hated by the Tzar, and that they would do well to drive him away. But his conduct had quite the opposite effect. The people in general, and the higher class of Belgrade citizens, thought that an insult to the King's father meant an insult to the King, and to insult the King of Servia was to insult the people of Servia. Belgrade society closed its doors against Mr. Jeadovsky. Of course, this did not matter much to him. But when, on the occasion of the national festival (February 22, 1899), all the foreign Ministers, and even Mr. Jeadovsky's two secretaries, had been invited to the diplomatic dinner in the Palace, with the sole exception of Mr. Jeadovsky himself, then it was evident that he could not any longer remain in Servia. The Russian Government recalled Mr. Jeadovsky.

CHAPTER XI

ATTEMPT ON THE LIFE OF KING MILAN

Dr. Vladan had published copies of several reports, which Mr. Jeadovsky, as the Russian Minister to Servia, sent from Belgrade to his chief, the Russian Minister for Foreign Affairs, Count Mouraviev. I have reason to know that there can be no doubt whatever that those are accurate copies of the originals.

They are simply full of stereotyped attacks on King Milan. They prove that Mr. Jeadovsky did not make independent observations of the facts by which he was surrounded in Belgrade, but thought it sufficient to echo all sorts of inventions, lies, and calumnies against King Milan, which specially paid journalists were instructed to spread in the European Press.

Not so much as a specimen of the style and character of this Russian diplomatist's despatches, but as an illustration of his recklessness and daring, I will quote here a passage from his despatch to Count Mouraviev, written on July 21, 1898 —

"The participation of King Milan in the Government, and his boundless influence on his weak-headed son, does not terrify me so much, because of his political convictions and his devotion to Austria, but because he lacks entirely all moral principle or simple honesty. He does not hesitate to exhibit ostentatiously this moral deficiency in the public and private relations of his life. This absence of elementary honesty permits us to say that he is ready, for the sake of his private interest, to throw Servia again into the abyss, and if a good opportunity presents itself, to sell Servia to anyone, leaving us again to re-purchase her at a very high price. Consequently, it seems to me to be absolutely necessary to save Servia; it is necessary in our own interest *that this evil should as soon as possible be cut down* (in the Russian 'presyetch')." See Dr. Vladan's *End of a Dynasty*, p.215.

What was in the mind of the Tzar's representative in Belgrade, when he thought it absolutely necessary that "this evil [namely, King Milan] should as soon as possible be cut down"? For the sake of human nature, and for the sake of the honour of the "Orthodox, Holy Russia," let us hope that that unfortunate phrase was not meant to mean what subsequent events led most people to believe it did mean.

On the 7th of November 1898, the Russian newspapers *Novoye Vremya* and *Novosti* brought news that reports were current that an attempt on the life of King Milan had been committed. Was that a *bona fide* false report? or was it an indiscreet echo of a certain resolution made in one or other of the Panslavonic circles, with which those papers were in touch?

On the 3rd of December 1898, the Servian newspaper *Srbobran*, which is published in Agram (Croatia), and was well known to be in touch with official and semi-official circles in St. Petersburg, published an article entitled "The Rupture between Russia and Obrenovich," in which it was said: "The present situation in Servia is very similar to one which prevailed in Bulgaria under Stambulov, and there is no doubt that it will be ended in the same way." As it is well known, Stambulov's anti-Russian regime in Bulgaria was ended by the assassination of Stambulov by a Russian hireling. The paper clearly announced that the anti-Russian Milan was to finish like the anti-Russian Stambulov.

The Russian paper *Le Nord*, which appears in the French language in Paris, published on the 9th (21st) February 1899, an alleged proclamation of the anti-dynastic Committee of the Servian Radical Party, "which warned the European capitalists not to lend money to Servia under Milan's regime, and refused responsibility for the crisis which, after the fall of Milan, would swallow all those who assisted him." Was it not strange that an organ of the Russian Foreign Office and *Le Nord* was well known to be such an organ should announce publicly that the fall of Milan was expected?

The above-mentioned paper *Srbobran*, in its issue of the 25th February 1899, commenting on the non-invitation of Jeadovsky to the diplomatic dinner at the Palace on the 22nd of that month, wrote: "Both Milan and his son will pay dearly for the insult to Jeadovsky. The departure of the Russian Minister from Servia will convince the people of Servia that they ought to destroy a regime which dares to provoke Russia."

All these extracts from the papers, well known to be at the disposal of the Russian Government (and which I take .from Dr. Vladan's book), show only the failure of the Russian Government to remove King Milan from Servia. The friends of King Milan, who knew that the Russian policy had no scrupulosity in choosing her methods and weapons to attain her objects, were earnestly anxious about his safety, especially since rumours were spread that the murderer of Stambulov, who freely moved in Sofia, visiting coffee-houses and places of amusement, openly boasted that he had obtained the mission to assassinate King Milan.

One day in the month of May the Servian Government received from Sofia a letter announcing that very soon a great crime would be committed in Belgrade, of which only the writer and two other persons had any knowledge. The writer was a certain Stephen, lately a servant in the Russian Legation in Belgrade, who was dismissed "because he was caught in stealing," as Colonel Taube, the Russian Military Agent, explained. The Servian Government offered to bring the man before the Court of Justice to be punished, if it should be proved that he had committed a theft. But Colonel Taube declined to prosecute him. He only desired that he should be expelled from Servia to Bulgaria, which was done by the Servian Government. Now his letter from Sofia, announcing that a crime was shortly to be committed in Belgrade, could not be, and was not, taken seriously by the Servian Government.

On the 21st June (Old Style) 1899, King Milan, accompanied by his Aide-de-Camp, Lukich, left shortly after 6 o'clock in the evening the Commander-in-Chiefs offices in the Citadel of Belgrade, driving in an open victoria to the Palace. Ten minutes later his carriage was just turning a corner to enter the principal street (Prince Michael's Street) leading from the Kalimegdan Park in front of the fortress, to the Palace, when a young man, standing in front of the corner house, a hotel with a coffee-house, fired a revolver at the King. After the first shot he ran after the carriage and fired three more shots. One bullet grazed King Milan's left shoulder, without causing a serious wound; but his Aide-de-Camp, Lukich, received a bullet in his shoulder.

In the confusion the would-be murderer ran down the sloping street to the shore of the Sava, and sprang into that river, but was captured and brought to the Prefecture. At the first examination by the Prefect, the prisoner declared that his name was Knezevich, that he was born in Bosnia, and his intention was to kill King Milan; his co-worker was the Colonel on the retired list, Vlayko Nicolich, and he obtained from the Prefect of Shabatz a pass for Roumania. In Bucharest he went to a certain house, where he met a gentleman, who spoke Servian, but with the Russian accent; and that gentleman, whose name he did not know, showed him a big bag of gold, and promised to give it to him if he killed King Milan. He gave him "on account" 500 napoleondors (£400), with which money he came to Belgrade, some eight days ago, to watch for an occasion to kill King Milan. He added that the gentleman accompanied him from Bucharest to Belgrade, and then recrossed the river to the Hungarian town, Zimony.

Two weeks later the house in which the Chief of the Russian Secret Police for Servia, Bulgaria, and Roumania lived in Bucharest, was photographed, and the photograph shown to the would-be assassin, Knezevich, who at once and before several witnesses recognised it as the house to which he went in Bucharest, and in which he met the man with the bag of gold. The photograph was certified by the Roumanian authorities to be the house in which the Russian Colonel M. lived.

The Prefect of Belgrade, Mr. Rista Bademlich, who made the first interrogatories with the would-be assassin Knezevich, in a private letter to Dr. Vladan, dated July 7th (19th) 1899, expressed his conviction that two Russian Colonels in official positions were at the head of the conspiracy to murder King Milan. The Prefect mentioned them by name, which names can be seen in Dr. Vladan's book, *The End of a Dynasty*, p.366.

The same authority asserts that a foreign minister in Bucharest, after the full investigation of the matter, reported to his Government that at the head of the conspiracy to murder King Milan were two Russian Colonels, whom he mentioned by name.

As King Milan escaped unhurt, the Russian Press-agents all over Europe, as well as in Servia, received instructions to inform the Press, that the attempt was nothing but a fraud, that King Milan himself had arranged this apparent conspiracy, and hired the *soi-disant* assassin; that, in fact, he made an attempt against himself, to gain an opportunity to denounce Russia, and imprison her devoted friends, the leaders of the Servian Radicals!

Unfortunately, King Alexander and King Milan played into the hands of their enemies. They committed a very grave fault by insisting that the Government should place Belgrade under martial law, arrest at once the members of the executive of the Radical Party, and place them together with Knezevich, as his instigators, before a Court-Martial. The Cabinet, under the leadership of Mr. Vukashin (in the absence of Dr. Vladan, who was taking the waters at Marienbad), after some show of resistance yielded to the pressure of both Kings. The Constitution of the year 1869, then in operation, allowed them to do so legally; but both morally and politically to bring the personal enemies of King Milan before a Court-Martial was a fatal mistake.

This extraordinary measure was disapproved by every right-thinking and independent man in Servia. It aroused the public opinion of Europe against the Servian Government and Servia. It was one of the misdeeds which told against King Alexander heavily. I consider it, and I deplore it, as one of the gravest mistakes which King Milan ever made.

The papers seized in the houses of the arrested leaders of the Radicals showed undoubtedly they met sometimes to discuss the political situation of the country, and that they in their confidential letters often expressed the desire, that the masterful bearing of King Milan should in some way or other be stopped, and even that they would be glad to see a change of dynasty; but there was no legal proof forthcoming that they had any connection with Knezevich's attempt on the life of King Milan. The Court-Martial, however, found that the attempt had some connection with the secret meetings and activity of the Radical leaders, and pronounced very severe sentences against them. Fortunately, the only man sentenced to death, and whose sentence was carried out, was Knezevich, who actually tried to kill King Milan.

In connection with the attempt on King Milan's life, and with the proclamation of the Court-Martial and condemnation of the Radical leaders, there exists a terrible insinuation.

It was made by King Milan, and King Alexander's Premier published it. Dr. Vladan not only published it, but in reporting the events, and especially the conversations which he himself or his locum tenens, Mr. Vukashin Petrovich, had with King Alexander at the time of the attempt and during the Court-Martial, he has drawn special attention to every action and every word of King Alexander which could give colour to the horrible accusation.

Not long before his death, King Milan told Dr. Vladan that he had reason to believe that the attempt on his life in June 1899 was instigated and organised by his own son Alexander, and his mistress, Draga Mashin, assisted by Russia!

King Milan was an exceedingly intelligent man, a very able controversialist, and a great casuist. Trained to be suspicious of everybody and of everything, and surrounded by men who often wished to exploit his suspiciousness, it is not extraordinary that sometimes he was led to exaggerate. If he had not been a King, he would have been a most able detective. Not rarely a small detail, which to all others would seem perfectly meaningless, to him was the starting point for the construction of most remarkable theories.

To illustrate this I will mention a case which concerned me personally. A great lover of flowers, I spoke on one occasion in 1886 with Queen Nathalie, in King Milan's presence, on roses. The Queen thereupon told Sasha to go and bring from her room three roses, and give them to me. A few weeks after that I read in a public sitting of our Academy a historical sketch of Princess Helene Balsha, who, in the beginning of the fifteenth century, as Regent for her young boy, reversed the policy of her late husband towards the republic of Venice, and tried to reconquer the towns which her husband had ceded to the Doge. At the time of my reading that paper King Milan was abroad. On his return to Belgrade I noticed that he treated me very coldly. As this lasted for some time, I asked him one day what it meant. "As you want to know what I have against you, I will tell it you frankly," began King Milan, evidently painfully agitated. "I have reason to believe that you are in conspiracy with the Queen and her friends to force me to abdicate and to proclaim her the Regent. My eyes were opened for the first time when she told Sasha to bring from her room those three roses, and give them to you. Those three roses meant, no doubt, the three members of the Regency, and there is a certain meaning even in the peculiar circumstance that Sasha, at her bidding, should place in your hands the emblem of the Regency! If I was willing to disbelieve the natural interpretation of the incident, your paper on Helene Balsha dispelled every doubt in me. The whole of your description of Helene is nothing but a glorification of Nathalie, the modern Helene Balsha! Practically your lecture before the Academy was nothing but the recommendation to the people to reconcile themselves with the Regency of Nathalie, who is known to hate my policy, as Helene Balsha disapproved of the policy of her husband!" The construction of such a theory was quite plausible. There were certainly some points of similarity between the situation of Helene Balsha and the situation of Queen Nathalie. Yet, at the same time, neither Queen Nathalie conspired to become the Regent for her son, nor had I ever thought, even for a moment, of such a contingency.

There is no doubt that King Alexander treated his father with great harshness, with monstrous callousness; but the accusation that he deliberately and in cold blood planned the assassination of his father, in order to remove the greatest obstacle to his marrying his mistress, cannot be accepted without positive and convincing proofs. Such proofs do not exist.

I wish also to draw attention to the fact that King Milan, with all his suspiciousness and detective ingenuity, did not suspect his son or his mistress of any foul play, either at the time of the attempt or a year afterwards. It was only after the harsh treatment he experienced from King Alexander on and after his marriage that his suspicions were aroused.

King Milan, Queen Nathalie and Prince Alexander, c.1880

King Milan and Prince Alexander, c.1888 (left)
Prince Alexander (right)

Ex-King Milan in later life (left)
Queen Nathalie (right)

King Alexander, c.1900 (left)
King Alexander and Queen Draga, c.1900 (right)

The wedding procession of King Alexander and Queen Draga at Belgrade, August 1900

Queen Draga in medieval costume, c.1900 (left)
Colonel Alexander Mashin (right)

Colonel Dragutin Dmitrijevic

The royal palace, Belgrade. The sovereigns' bodies were thrown from the open window at centre

A contemporary artist's impression of the bodies being thrown from the palace window

*An In Memoriam postcard published after the murders of
the King and Queen*

The tomb of the sovereigns, St Mark's Church, Belgrade

CHAPTER XII

ON THE EVE OF THE FATAL DEED

In March 1900 I was transferred from London to Constantinople as the Servian Envoy Extraordinary and Minister Plenipotentiary.

Passing through Vienna I went to pay my respects to Count Goluchowsky, whose personal acquaintance I made in Paris in 1882, and renewed (1894) it in Bucharest, where at that time the Count represented Austro-Hungary, while I acted as the Servian Minister to the Roumanian Court.

Before leaving Count Goluchowsky I asked his Excellency if he had a message for King Alexander and King Milan.

"Yes, certainly," answered the Count. "Tell their Majesties that it is really most important, indeed most urgent, that King Alexander should not delay any longer his marriage. He is exposed to serious personal danger as long as he has no heir to the throne. We wish to see the political consolidation of Servia, which cannot be realised while the Royal dynasty has only one representative. King Alexander, highly intelligent as he is, seems to be perfectly aware that his first duty to his dynasty, and to his people, is to marry without any further delay. When I saw him here the last time, he expressed the hope and the wish that his Majesty, my august master, would help him to obtain the hand of a suitable Princess. You can tell him from me that not only his Majesty the Emperor and the King interests himself personally in his happiness, but also the Emperor of Germany joined our Kaiser in efforts to find for King Alexander a suitable Princess. But your King makes too many conditions and claims. He says the Princess must be young, beautiful, and lovely, so as to win his love; further, she ought to be politically well connected, and at least have family relations with one of the first-class Courts of Europe; further, she ought to be a highly cultured and gifted woman; and, last but not least, very wealthy. Please tell the King that a Princess who possesses all these conditions could do better than marry King Alexander of Servia and spend her life in Belgrade! Therefore, he ought to be satisfied if we succeed in finding for him a Princess who possesses some of his stipulations. And, thanks to the interest which the Emperor William takes in the matter, I think we are in a position to recommend to him one of the most charming and most cultured Princesses in Europe."

On my arrival in Belgrade I was immediately invited to dine at the Palace. After dinner King Alexander took his father, King Milan, his Premier Dr. Vladan, and myself into the central salon of the Old Palace to have a private talk. I immediately delivered Count Goluchowsky's message, and added my own arguments in support of the Count's contention that it was really of the highest importance that the King should speedily be married.

Both King Milan and the Premier were highly pleased with Count Goluchowsky's message. King Milan asked me if the Count divulged to me who the Princess was. He was pleased to hear that he did not. "But, of course," he added, "we know whom he meant; and I think Sasha admits that according to her photograph she must be a lovely young woman."

"According to her photograph, certainly," repeated King Alexander, who until that moment had been silent, absorbed in deep thought, drinking his mocha and smoking a cigarette. "Certainly; but you know I cannot decide before I have seen her personally. You do not know, Mijatovich, but I may tell you, that Vladan has made me an ultimatum, declaring that he will resign his post and leave me if I do not marry this year. I promised him, as well as papa, that I would do so. And I mean to keep my word."

He spoke with much calmness, and with such apparent assurance and sincerity, that Dr. Vladan seemed happy. King Milan (who was walking restlessly near the Turkish, low coffee-table, around which we sat on low arm-chairs) came straight to his son, and kissed him tenderly. I felt really moved, and was happy too. I could not dream that the young King was only acting and deceiving us all three, as if we were innocent babes, or stupid and blind idiots.

"But, of course," King Alexander continued, "some delay is unavoidable. Papa must now go first to take a cure at Carlsbad. You think he looks well, but in truth he is ill. He hardly eats anything, and he must go to Carlsbad. And as you see, Dr. Vladan has made a wreck of himself in untiring service to his King and country, and he wants to go to Franzensbad. Now, we three cannot be absent from Servia at the same time. Therefore, we have arranged that papa and Vladan go first to make their respective cures; Vladan will then make a trip to Paris to see the exhibition. On his return to Belgrade I join papa in Vienna, go with him to Paris, and then to Germany to see my Princess, and, if God so wills, give her the ring; and certainly by the end of the year, if not sooner, you will see me a married man."

About the middle of April 1900, the Servian Minister in Berlin, Mr. Milan Boghitchevich, a relative of the Obrenovich House, reported to the Servian Minister of Foreign Affairs, Dr. Vladan, that on April 13th he saw Count Bülow on some official business of minor importance, and that the Count on that occasion mentioned that it was time for the King of Servia to marry, as the Royal dynasty consisted only of King Alexander and his father King Milan. Mr. Boghitchevich reported further that he gave a rather evasive answer, saying that from what he knew it seemed that King Alexander had as yet no intention of marrying. Dr. Vladan was exceedingly astonished, and asked the Minister to explain what on earth was his reason for such an evasive answer. In his private letter to Dr. Vladan, dated Berlin, 27th April, 1900, Mr. Boghitchevich writes —

"These are my reasons why I gave such an evasive answer to Count Bülow. Nearly two years ago his Majesty the King instructed me to make certain inquiries about a German Princess, who is related to several European Courts, and whose sister is already a Queen. The Emperor of Germany takes great interest in her, because his own sister had married into her family. Last year the Emperor said to me once, and to my wife several times, that the Princess would be a good match for our King. I reported it to his Majesty our King, but had very little success. When Count Bülow lately spoke to me about the desirability that our King should marry, I knew that he had this same Princess in view. Having obtained information about the inclinations of our King in that respect, I dared not give any other but an evasive answer, as I had no instruction to speak either for or against it. I thought it wise to prepare Count Bülow for the eventuality that King Alexander might decide not to marry the Princess. The best proof that the King does not mean to marry her is the fact that as yet he has never spoken to you about it," etc. etc.

This letter alarmed somewhat Dr. Vladan. He went at once to King Alexander with Mr. Boghitchevich's two letters, as well as with his own, showed them to the King, and asked for information.

The King explained. Two years ago his cousin Milan Boghitchevich bothered him so much with suggestions that he should marry a certain German Princess that, to get rid of his importunities, he ordered him to make certain preliminary inquiries, but nothing more. But Boghitchevich went beyond his instructions; and especially his wife, who went even so far as to decide the Emperor to honour in view of the approaching alliance the concert which the Servian Singing Society of Belgrade gave in Berlin. He King Alexander considered this only as a simple courtesy of the Kaiser, who, as is well known, delights in showing courtesies. However that may be, it was now the time to act earnestly, and he could most positively assure his dear Premier, that within three, or at the latest four months, his marriage would be an accomplished fact.

Dr. Vladan was perfectly satisfied with this explanation.

The very next day after this conversation between King Alexander and Dr. Vladan his Premier, the Prefect of the Police of Belgrade, Mr. Rista Bademlich, came as usual very early, to show to the Premier the police report prepared for the King. Having delivered his usual report, he startled Dr. Vladan by suddenly saying —

"I say, Mr. President, my 'Kooma' will cause us a terrible misfortune."

"Which Kooma[1] do you mean?"

Bademlich: "You know I mean that misfortune-bringing woman, Draga Mashin."

Dr. Vladan: "But why should that person bring us misfortune. What interest could she have in doing so?"

Bademlich: "She has made the King perfectly blind, so that he cannot see anything but her; and spends every night with her. Do you not know that she has, with the magic drinks she gives him, made him so foolish that he spends hours under her window, begging her humbly to let him in? Have you never thought that the King, when waiting under Draga's windows in that otherwise deserted street,

---

1 "Kooma" in feminine, "Koom" in masculine form, are the Servian names for principal witnesses at a wedding, as well as for the godmothers and godfathers.

might be murdered, or catch a serious illness, in wet and cold weather."

Dr. Vladan: "We know all that."

Bademlich: "And yet you take no steps to stop this shame and scandal."

Dr. Vladan: "We do not undertake anything, because if we tried, he would rightly stop us by saying that our duty is to attend to State business, and not to his personal and private love-making; and that he does not prevent us taking the necessary measures for his safety, which is the duty of the Home Minister, and your own, my dear Prefect of the Police! Besides, as I am informed, the King is always, on such visits, accompanied by Colonel Marko, whose sword and revolver are worth as much as a squadron of guards, which, of course, could not accompany the King to the windows of Draga. You ought, however, to place always in the neighbourhood a sufficient number of detectives, who could rush at the first shrill whistle of Colonel Marko to his orders."

Dr. Vladan tried, without much pruderie, to explain why the Government allowed King Alexander to have a mistress. The arguments are too physiological and cynical to be repeated in decent society. In addition, he thought that as the relations between Alexander and Draga had lasted now several years, it gave grounds to believe that the King would probably tire of his nine or ten years' older mistress, and that he would soon give her up. He had not the slightest doubt that would be the case the moment the King married the young and charming Princess, whom he the King had in view. After the long dissertation of Dr. Vladan, the Prefect Bademlich asked Bademlich: "Mr. President, do you and your colleagues really believe that the King will marry according to our hopes and wishes, so long as he has Draga?"

Dr. Vladan: "I am sure of it. On New Year's Day the King gave me, in the presence of his father, the Ministers and the State dignitaries, in the most solemn way, his Royal word that, in the course of the year, he would marry."

Bademlich: "And I say to you, Mr. President, and I beg you to mark my words: this woman has bewitched the King so completely that he firmly believes that with no other woman could he ever be happy indeed, that to no other woman could he ever be a husband! And if the King means to keep his word, which he so solemnly gave to you, he means, simply, to marry Draga Mashin!"

Dr. Vladan (loudly laughing): "What do you say? Draga Mashin a Queen of Servia? Listen, my dear fellow, what you have just said is too strong. You are such an excellent Police Prefect that I cannot understand how such folly could have ever entered your head, and much less how you could give expression to it. It is evident that you do not know anything of the science of psychology, and especially that you are not acquainted with the psychology of sovereigns."

Bademlich: "Well; but I tell you one thing — I would not give my *praktik* (he used that word), for all your *grammatik*, or whatever your scientific theories might be called. I warn you, Mr. President, to take care that you do not one day repent having relied too much on your science! Then it will be too late for you, for us all, and for the country!"

Three months later, events proved that the practical common-sense of an experienced police officer had been far more clear-sighted than the psychology and physiology of the learned Dr. Vladan.

Dr. Vladan — from whose Memoirs I have taken the report of his conversation with Bademlich — acknowledges that himself. He, however, explains his mistake by saying that he assumed quite normal conditions in King Alexander, whereas the autopsy after the catastrophe proved that Alexander was not normally constituted.

On June 6th (19th), 1900, King Alexander told Dr. Vladan that his father, King Milan, would leave Belgrade for Carlsbad the next day, with a special mission to stay first for a few days in Vienna, to speak with the Emperor of Austria concerning his (King Alexander's) marriage. Dr. Vladan expressed his great pleasure in hearing this.

"Well, then," continued the King, "you must do me a pleasure, too. It is very probable that I shall have to leave Belgrade, even before my birthday, August 2nd (14th), to go to Carlsbad, not to the cure, but to meet my intended. You will admit yourself that it is highly desirable that we should meet to see if — putting all other conditions aside — we could have that sympathy for each other that is absolutely needful, even in a marriage made from the 'highest State reasons.' But I cannot leave the country before you and papa return. You have not only to make your cure at Marienbad, but also to go to Paris to see our Pavilion at the Exhibition. You will want six or seven weeks for all that. I think it, therefore, desirable that you start at once on your leave of absence."

Dr. Vladan expressed his willingness to leave for Vienna on the 8th, that is in two days."

"Thank you, Doctor!" said the King, with a deep sigh, as if he suddenly were relieved from a great weight. "Only, please don't forget what I told you about the special mission of my father to Vienna must remain a secret. I beg of you not to show in conversation with my father that you know anything about it. Because if he does not succeed, it might not be pleasant for him to learn that besides the Emperor and us, someone else was in the secret. When you see Goluchowsky, there is no need for you to take the initiative in talking with him on my marriage. But if he speaks to you on the subject, I authorise you to ask him for his support in the matter."

On June 7th (20th), King Milan left Belgrade for Vienna. The next day the Premier, Dr. Vladan, having given over his duties as President of the Cabinet and Foreign Minister to his colleague, the Minister of Finance, Vukashin Petrovich, left also for Vienna.

King Alexander, Draga Mashin, and the Russian Chargé d'Affaires, Mr. Mansuroff, had now a clear field to themselves.

CHAPTER XIII

ALEXANDER'S MARRIAGE WITH DRAGA MASHIN

On Thursday, July 6th (19th), 1900, there was in the afternoon the usual reception of the foreign diplomats in the Servian Foreign Office in Belgrade. The last Minister to be received was the German Minister, Baron Waecker-Gotter. The *locum tenens* of the Servian Premier and Foreign Minister, Mr. Vukashin Petrovich, was just leaving the building, together with the Baron, when the Home Minister, Mr. George Genchich, stopped him, and asked him to return at once with him to his office. He said to him, in a visible state of agitation —

"I cannot tell you what it is, but I will only say, something fateful, something fatal, something dreadful is going to happen! I was obliged to take an oath that I should not betray the secret, and I shall not do so. But this I can tell you, that I have wired in cipher to King Milan, that a great misfortune for him personally, for King Alexander, for Servia, and for us all is in preparation, and have asked him to come at once to prevent that misfortune, if possible."

Mr. Genchich advised his colleague to go to the Palace at once. "Perhaps the King will tell you what is going on."

It was nearly 7 o'clock p.m. Mr. Petrovich — whom I shall call Mr. Vukashin, as he always signs himself, and as he is generally known in Servia under that name went to the Palace, and was surprised to find in the antechamber old Mr. Nicholas Christich waiting. Mr. Christich had been generally called to the Palace during the last thirty years whenever the Kings of Servia found themselves in an exceptionally difficult situation. Mr. Vukashin asked the old statesman laughingly —

"Have you perhaps come to form a new Cabinet?"

King Alexander received Mr. Vukashin in great agitation and irritation. He told him simply that he had then no time to listen to him, and dismissed him somewhat ungraciously, in a few minutes. The Minister felt so humiliated and offended that he went home and wrote his resignation.

On July 7th (20th), Dr. Vladan, on his journey from Zurich to Lucerne, received a telegram from his *locum tenens*, Vukashin, stating that he had resigned, and begging him to return at once. Vladan wired to King Milan at Carlsbad, and asked him if he knew what was taking place in Belgrade. Dr. Vladan and King Milan wired that day to each other in ciphers, but they could not decipher their despatches with the cipher books which King Alexander's Secretary had given them. Losing much precious time in unsuccessful deciphering, both were annoyed; but they did not suspect that by the King's order they were given wrong books. Even this small detail was foreseen! At last, on July 8th (21st), King Milan wired to Dr. Vladan, in an open telegram, that he had received from the Home Minister, Genchich, an urgent request to return at once to Servia, "but secretly." "To return secretly was not compatible with my duty. I therefore refused the request, and asked for information by a letter."

A little later on the same day, Dr. Vladan received in Lucerne the following telegram —

"The King has decided to marry Draga Mashin. The Government has resigned, feeling unable to prevent that catastrophe for the country and dynasty. — VUKASHIN."

Dr. Vladan wired to King Alexander in cipher —

"Vukashin announces to me, by a telegram of this day, that your Majesty has decided to marry Mme. Draga Mashin. Most humbly I pray your Majesty to let me know if this fatal decision for Servia and for the dynasty was a definite one."

King Alexander answered the same day, in a telegram which had only two ciphers, which meant —

"Yes, my decision is definite. — ALEXANDER."

On the same day Dr. Vladan received two other telegrams. The one was from Carlsbad —

"I have sent in my resignation as Commander-in-Chief of the Army, but you do not resign at least for a day or two. If possible, come at once to me. — MILAN."

The other telegram was from Belgrade, signed by Mr. Vukashin —

"The question is decided. The resignation of the Cabinet has been accepted."

Dr. Vladan, having ceased to be the head of the Government, thought it useless to go to Carlsbad to confer with King Milan, who had ceased to be the head of the Servian Army.

The foregoing story is only a chronological sketch of the events which rapidly followed each other. I now raise the curtain to depict a drama. The diary, or rather the memorandum, which has been written by one of the principal actors of the drama itself, gives us a graphic description of the events.[1]

On July 7th (20th), early in the morning, King Alexander had in his hands the resignation of his Acting Premier, Mr. Vukashin; but he returned it to him, and invited him to lunch. Everybody in the Palace noticed that the King was that morning somewhat preoccupied, irritable, and confused. After the luncheon he took Mr. Vukashin to a small but elegantly furnished room in the Palace, known as Queen Nathalie's Boudoir.

The King: "I have something of the greatest importance to tell you, something on which depend my future, my life, my destiny. But let me in the first place reproach you for your resignation. We have been so many years such good friends that we have no right to be over-sensitive in small matters. Have you seen Genchich? Has he told you anything?"

The Minister: "Yes, I have seen Genchich; but, unfortunately he refused to tell me anything."

The King: "Well, then, I will presently tell you everything myself; but before we do so, you must make a solemn oath on this holy picture, that you will not tell anyone what I am now going to confide to you!"

And with those words King Alexander brought out from his breast a small bijou holy eikon of the Russian type, which of late he had taken to wearing on a gold chain. Probably the picture represented Saint Nicholas, the patron saint of the family Obrenovich. I believe it was the gift of his mistress Draga, and very likely she made it doubly precious to him by swearing on it to love him, and to be faithful to him through all eternity.

---

1 The Diary of Vukashin Petrovich, Minister of Finance in the Cabinet of Dr. Vladan, and his locum tenens in the Premiership and the Foreign Office during his absence. Printed in Dr. Vladan's book, *The End of a Dynasty*, pp. 559-588.

The Minister: "Your Majesty, I must tell you that I do not believe in holy pictures, and an oath on them would not be binding on me."

The King: "Then swear by the memory of your departed son."

Mr. Vukashin Petrovich had a very gifted and promising son, a young doctor, who a year or two before these events died in a Vienna hospital from blood-poisoning, through a wound got in a surgical operation.

The Minister: "The memory of my son is certainly sacred to me, but I cannot make it the foundation for an oath."

The King: "Then give me your word of honour."

The Minister: "Certainly; but only after I have seen that my word of honour will not bring me into conflict with my other duties."

The King rose in evident anger, and with the words: "In that case I have nothing to tell you," left the room.

But in ten minutes he returned, went near Mr. Vukashin and said: "Why should you not promise me to keep the secret?"

The Minister: "My refusal concerns only the secrets of the State; but if you have to tell me something that does not concern the State and public service, you may be sure that I will carry it with me to the grave."

The King: "Very well. Now, listen to me. You know, Vukashin, that I have had neither childhood nor youth like other men. The eternal quarrel between my parents made my life bitter, undermined my health in general, and my nerves more especially. Such a life killed in me every sentiment. I have never had any ambition, not even the ambition to reign as a King. I wear the crown, not because I love it, but because it is my duty to do so. You must have noticed that yourself."

The Minister: "In what you say, Sire, is certainly some truth, but as you have touched upon delicate family relations I cannot say anything about them."

The King: "Very well. Hear only what I have further to say. You and your colleagues have always pressed me to marry. I have now decided to do what you have wished. Having come to this decision, I found that none of the great Sovereign Courts was willing to give me one of their daughters for wife. No Princess belonging to a great dynasty is willing to marry me. Indeed, it would be foolish for anyone to give up her fine life in her own country and exchange it for the life in Servia. I am really not disposed to marry a Princess belonging to a branch line and to a little Court; and, besides, such a marriage would bring to our people no advantage. A foreign Princess from a small Court would try to exercise influence on the business of the State. That would without fail cause dissatisfaction in the country, and put me, personally, in a very awkward position. Therefore, I have decided to marry a Servian, a daughter of my own people. What do you say to that, Vukashin?"

The Minister: "Personally, Sire, I have no aristocratic prejudices, and am more with the democratic tendencies of our time. And, therefore — although for different reasons and not for those you adduce — I have nothing against the marriage of your Majesty with a Servian, provided that she is from a respectable house, well educated, young, at least five years younger than your Majesty, and pure as an angel. Such a Queen could gain the love of the people. Such a Queen the Servians would really prefer to a foreign Princess, and your Government would not oppose the wish of your Majesty."

The King (rising up): "Yes, but all the difficulty lies just therein, that there exists already a woman, whom I love more than anyone or anything in this world, the only woman with whom I can be perfectly happy, and only then can I consecrate my whole life to the interests of the people if she becomes my wife. In the whole world there is only one woman who can make me forget the bitterness of my past life, and make me feel happy. That woman has been hitherto my good angel, who gave me strength to bear patiently all that I had to bear."

The Minister: "And who is that woman, Sire?"

The King: "That woman is — Madame Draga, the daughter of the late Panta Lunyevitza."

The Minister (in consternation): "Draga Mashin? . . . No, Sire, that cannot be — that ought not to be."

The King's eyes filled with tears, not of tender emotion, but of rage. He took off his binocle, rubbed it spasmodically with his handkerchief, fixed them again on the bridge of his nose, bit the ends of his moustache, jumped from his seat, walked hurriedly **about the room, sat down again, and again jumped up and walked** nervously about. At last he stopped before the Minister, and said —

The King: "Are you my friend, Vukashin?"

The Minister: "That I am, Sire."

The King: "If you are my friend, you ought to help me to carry out my purpose. It cannot be otherwise. From this my purpose I will not desist, whatever may happen; and he who tries to hinder me is my enemy."

The Minister: "That being so, I lose no time in declaring that I cease to be your Majesty's Minister."

After some conversation between the King and the Minister concerning the course which the King might follow in forming a new Cabinet, the Minister, according to his Diary, reverted to the communication the King had made to him.

The Minister: "I pray your Majesty most graciously to forgive me if I say anything that a Minister who has just resigned ought not to say. It is hard for me to believe that you mean to marry Madame Draga. Do you not see, Sire, that such a step is nothing less than the suicide of the dynasty? Putting aside anything that could be said against that lady, her known sterility would be quite sufficient to prove what I have just said. But other circumstances of the case ought not to be overlooked. Madame Draga is much older than yourself. She does not enjoy a good reputation — rightly or wrongly — and as it often happens in common life, a good mistress does not make always a good wife. The Pretender Peter Karageorgevich would gain, in consequence of such a marriage, much more than if he had distributed a million napoleondors to the agitators against the Obrenovich Dynasty. You ought to know, Sire, that after such a marriage not a single European Court will receive you; you will be boycotted by all the Sovereigns in Europe. The entire intelligence of the country will rebel against it, and will never be reconciled to it. Not only your Majesty, but Servia will lose the esteem which it now enjoys in the world, and will soon become an object of irony and contempt. Believe me, Sire, I would gladly sacrifice my life if I could but save you from this fatal step — "

The King (interrupting him): "Hear me once for all, Vukashin. I am inflexibly resolved to marry Madame Draga. Don't insult me by attacks on her. She is an honest and honourable woman; and only her enemies speak badly of her. The difference in the ages is not so great. She is only eight years older than I, and you know how often such cases take place amongst our people. Of course, I know that the enemies of our dynasty will exploit this opportunity against us, as they would any other. You say you speak to me as a friend; but you will allow me that I have my own convictions. Your opinion is based on a hypothesis; my own is founded on facts and proofs."

After a silence of a few minutes the King continued —

"I will give you at once the proof that Draga is an honest and honourable woman. I made her acquaintance in 1894. Her modesty, her wisdom, her entire bearing pleased me much, and impressed me deeply. I took every opportunity to approach her. She persistently evaded me. When at last I succeeded in entering her room, she protested most energetically; and when I declared to her that without her I could not live, she simply took me by the shoulders and pushed me — her King — outside. I say that only an honest and honourable woman could act thus. All the time she lived at Biarritz she did not permit me to come near her. Much later, after she came to Belgrade, and after she got proofs that without her and her love I could not live, has she sacrificed herself for me. Yes, I am passionately in love with her, and without her I cannot live!"

The Minister, using cleverly the intimate confessions which the King had just made to him, suggested that he should at least adjourn his marriage with Draga for a year, employing that time to the restoration of his health. But the King laughed with scorn at the cautious Minister's suggestion. The Minister asked him if he had informed his father, King Milan, of his decision.

"No," answered the King, "as yet I have not told him anything. But there is now no power on earth which could prevent my marrying Draga, whatever the consequences may be! I would prefer to give up my crown, and live with Draga on a revenue of 9000 francs (£360) a year, than possess the crown and a Civil-list of 1,200,000 francs (£48,000). Whatever I had I have given her. I gave her 500,000 francs that she should not leave me. I knew that my marriage with her would meet with extraordinary difficulties; therefore, I have surrendered myself to her, body and soul, and, therefore, I have made it impossible for her to leave me. You ought to know that she persistently refused to become Queen. I alone know what difficulties I have had to gain her consent. And now, after I have at last broken down her resistance, you come and make difficulties! Have you no pity for me? Do you wish to force me to go away for ever? Because you ought to be perfectly certain that, if I cannot marry Draga as King, I will leave Servia for ever, and marry her as a private individual."

The conversation was here broken off. He told Vukashin that he would be engaged for an hour, but that he (the Minister) must not leave the Palace until his return. Practically he arrested the Minister.

The King went, accompanied by an Equerry, to Draga's little house, and spent some time with her. On his return to the Palace, he allowed the Premier to leave; but ordered him to come early next day with all his colleagues.

He called then his private secretary, Dr. Voislav Velykovich, and asked him to help him to write a proclamation, in which he announced to the people his engagement to Draga. Dr. Velykovich refused, and then and there resigned his post. A violent scene took place between them. At last they came to a compromise; the King accepted the resignation of his private secretary. Dr. Velykovich remained his old friend, and assisted the King to compose his proclamation to the people of Servia.

The next day, Saturday, July 8th (21st), all the Ministers, at a Cabinet Council, wrote and signed their collective resignations. In that document they stated that, after all their efforts to decide his Majesty to give up his fatal intention of marrying Mme. Draga Mashin had been unsuccessful, there remained nothing to them but to request his Majesty to accept their resignations.

At the same time the Cabinet decided to take an important step. The Minister of Public Works, Colonel Borivoy, and the Minister for Home Affairs, Genchich, were sent to Mme. Draga Mashin. In the name of the Government they represented to her that her marriage with the King would cause the ruin of the dynasty, and be a great misfortune to the country. They appealed to her love for the King and the country, and begged her to do them both a signal service by preventing that marriage, and hinted that the country would liberally recompense her for such a service. They asked her to leave the country at once. I do not know if Mr. Genchich told her that in the case of her refusal, she would, that very morning, be forcibly carried out of the country.

Mme. Draga listened to them with great calmness, and apparently agreed fully with their ideas. She said she was ready to leave the country, but she must have at least a few hours to pack up. While her maid did this, she would hide herself in the house of an intimate friend, where the King could not discover her. And she left her house in a carriage.

Draga proved herself a very able actress on that occasion. She succeeded in misleading the Ministers concerning her sincerity. If she had refused to comply with their suggestion, she would have been most probably carried away forcibly across the river to Hungary. But she complied readily. At the same time, to her younger brother, who put her in the carriage, she whispered the name of the friend to whom she was going.

Two hours later, King Alexander came to see Draga. He got into a rage when he found that she had left, and that no one in the house knew where she had gone. Her brother professed ignorance, but after some time, yielding to the pressing questions of the enraged King, he confided to him his sister's hiding-place. The King drove at once to the house of Draga's friend, and brought her back to her own home; and then and there put on her finger a beautiful diamond ring, declaring himself formally engaged to her.

So failed miserably the only attempt of the Government to frustrate the marriage of King Alexander with Draga.

It is true they sent also the Minister of Education and Church Affairs to the Archbishop of Belgrade and the Metropolitan of Servia, to draw his attention to the terrible consequences for the dynasty, Servia, and for himself personally, if he dared to give his blessing to such a marriage. But the Archbishop Inokentiye was well known as the most unreliable of men. He did try to persuade the King to give it up, but soon perceived that all his efforts were useless.

The Acting-Premier Vukashin states in his Diary that he had one moment the idea to arrest the King in the Palace, or to carry him forcibly out of the country! He asked the War Minister, General Atanaskovich, if such a plan could be successfully executed. The General answered that he could do it, but that he would not, because such an act would demoralise all discipline in the army. Naturally, Mr. Vukashin had to give up his idea, and ask his colleague to promise him never to mention it to anyone.

King Alexander's proclamation, announcing to the people his engagement with Draga Mashin, created consternation among the true friends of the Obrenovich Dynasty, and generally produced the greatest impression and astonishment in the country.

The most intimate friends of the King, who had free access to the Palace, implored him to desist from his fatal intention. The King refused to receive most of them. Those whom he received were told that, if they were really his friends, they ought to help him to achieve the only desire of his heart, to marry the only woman whom he loved with all his heart and soul, and who alone was able to make him happy. It was no use to talk to him of consequences, he was ready to take all the consequences; and his determination to marry Draga was unalterable and inflexible.

A deputation of influential citizens, most of them well known as the dynasty's devoted friends, asked for an audience, and were received. Led by Michael Pavlovich and Marko Vuletich, they frankly acquainted the King of most deplorable impressions created everywhere by his engagement to Draga Mashin. Some of them even hinted that rumours were circulating concerning the lady's reputation. The King warmly defended his fiancée, assured them that he knew her to be a perfectly honourable woman, that she was his guardian-angel, that she was a true Servian woman, and a great patriot, and that in the end, whatever she was or is, she was the only woman he loved, or could love; and that he would rather lose his throne and crown, yes, even his life, than live without her love. The deputations left the Palace deeply distressed. Some of them thought the young King talked and behaved as if he were bewitched.

The town was full of all sorts of rumours. One of them was that the officers of the Belgrade garrison, perfectly disgusted that their King should marry his mistress, had decided to go together to the Palace and ask the King either to give up his mad intention, or abdicate in favour of his father.

The difficulty of the situation was dangerously complicated by the inability of the King to form a new Cabinet. All the more important politicians, well known as devoted friends of the dynasty, refused to form a new Government. All the public services seemed disorganised, and everything was unsettled. The friends of the dynasty expected every moment to hear that King Milan had crossed the frontier to Servia, or that the officers had forced the King either to give up Draga or the throne. King Alexander never vacillated for a moment in his determination, but was physically nearly exhausted, and quite in despair, when a telegram was brought to him. His face brightened, he sighed deeply, as a man who suddenly is relieved of a terribly oppressive weight. Later in the day he received the Russian Charge d' Affaires, Mansuroff. The official Gazette brought, printed in thick letters, the following Court communication:—

"*Belgrade, July* 13, 1900. At the order of his Imperial Majesty, Tzar Nicholas II., the Imperial Russian Chargé d'Affaires, Monsieur Paul Mansuroff, visited, to-day, his Majesty the King, and, in the name of his exalted sovereign, congratulated him on his engagement. Immediately after, the Chargé d'Affaires went to visit the Serene fiancée of the King, Madame Draga, to express to her his good wishes.'

The Russians had taken care throughout the last fifty years to educate the poor Servians to look on Russia as the Holy Orthodox country, on the Tzar as the permanent protector, and the only true friend of the Servian people. At the bidding of Russia, the predominant political party, the Radicals, did everything to embitter the life of King Milan, and drive him from the throne. At this critical moment for the dynasty and for Servia, Russia gave a sign to her friends that the marriage of King Alexander with Draga Mashin should be accepted. All good Servians, all good orthodox people, who had perhaps hesitated, ought to follow the example of the great friend of the Servians, the great orthodox Tzar of all the Russias. Not only did he congratulate King Alexander and his fiancée Draga, but he formally accepted the sacred functions of the "Koom" at their wedding. There was not — nor could any longer be — the slightest doubt that Russia, in the person of Tzar Nicholas II, highly approved of the marriage of King Alexander with Draga Mashin. More than that, the Tzar had accepted to be the principal co-operator and co-officiator at the church ceremony of the wedding. This was regarded with disgust by those Servians who firmly believed that the fatal marriage of Alexander with Draga was entirely the work of Russia, which thereby wanted to definitely close the door of Servia to her hated enemy, Milan, even if she thereby should risk the ruin of the dynasty Obrenovich.

About the same time, when the Tzar's demonstration in favour of Alexander's marriage with Draga had broken the resistance of his true friends, the Continental papers published the following letter, written by poor King Milan, to his beloved son:

* * * * * * *

"MY *DEAR SON*, — With the best will to oblige you, I cannot give my consent to the impossible marriage for which you have decided. You ought to know that, by doing what you intend, you are pushing Servia into an abyss. Our dynasty has sustained many a blow, and has continued to live. But this blow would be so terrible that the dynasty could never recover from it. You have still time to think it over. If your decision should really be, as you say, inflexible, then, nothing remains for me but to pray to God for our fatherland. I shall be the first to cheer the Government

which shall drive you from the country, after such a folly on your part. —
Your father, MILAN."

CHAPTER XIV

KING ALEXANDER AND THE SERVIAN ARMY

King Alexander had no natural predisposition to be a soldier, and he really never was a soldier. Perhaps his short-sightedness, from which he suffered from childhood, was the principal cause. In his education they tried to instil in him the military spirit. But with no success. He was a politician and not a soldier. He disliked to wear the uniform of an officer, and preferred to dress in mufti.

King Milan was also far more a politician than a soldier; but he was aware of the essential importance of the devotion of the army to the throne and to the dynasty, and did everything to secure its devotion and loyalty. As the Commander-in-Chief he really did great things for the efficiency of the army, and identified himself entirely with the officers, and certainly was very popular with them. King Alexander was never able to inspire confidence and devotion. During the time King Milan was at the head of the army it was loyal to the dynasty; but even though no officer showed an enthusiastic devotion to King Alexander personally, he was neither exactly liked nor disliked.

But since his marriage with Draga Mashin King Alexander became decidedly unpopular with the army. His marriage with a simple Servian woman, who was well known to have been his mistress for several years, and about whom all sorts of scandalous stories were in circulation — particularly among the officers — alienated from him even that little sympathy and devotion which he possessed in the army. His harsh and contemptuous treatment of officers, who came to the Palace to implore him to give up his intention of marrying Draga, had offended many of them bitterly. And the order which he gave to some of his Court officers, as, for instance, to Colonel Kumrich, to fire on his father Milan and kill him "as a mad dog," if he should attempt to cross into Servia, filled them almost all with amazement and horror.

About the relations of King Alexander to the Servian Officers, Mr. Pera Todorovich has published a very characteristic conversation which he had with the King only a few months before the catastrophe. The King wanted to hear from this devoted friend of his father and his own — who certainly had one of the finest political intelligences among all the politicians of Servia — what he, with his great knowledge of the people, thought about the chances of the Pretender Prince Peter Karageorgevich. After some talk, King Alexander said that the impressions which his friend received in the country, and his own personal convictions were, that Karageorgevich had no chance as a really dangerous pretender to the throne of Servia.

"I beg your pardon, Sire," interrupted Mr. Todorovich, "what I meant to say is this: *Karageorgevich has just as many chances as you yourself give him!* The success of his partisans is dependent on your own want of success, their progress on your losses, mistakes, and errors. Whatever you neglect or give up they will cultivate and try to win to their cause; who you alienate they will try at once to draw towards their pretender. Owing to this, I have the greatest anxiety about the army. Excuse me, your Majesty, do not take it badly from me, nor be annoyed about what I am going to say: you are neglecting the army, and you have, in one sense, given it entirely up!"

The King flushed and snorted. He did not like it. Excitedly he said —

"How have I given it up? When, where, and how have I neglected it? . . . That is only an artificial cry. Come here, and show me where I have neglected the army."

"Wherein have you neglected it? . . . I cannot prove that better than by asking you to compare your own treatment of the army with the manner in which your father King Milan treated it. Compare what he had done for the army, with what you have done, and you will then see clearly the great difference."

"But what is wrong in my treatment of the army? . . . I do for the army all I can. I deprive other branches of the public service of what is their due, that the army should have more than enough. If there are promotions, they are in the army; if there are decorations by orders and prizes, the army has them; and if the public treasury has money or not, the army must have it. If I have ever done or given anything to anyone it has been to the army. And now you want me to do still more. Tell me openly, express yourself clearly, wherein you find fault with me. . . . You mention to me King Milan. But King Milan was a clever actor. I do not understand the art of playing a studied part; it is not in my nature."

He spoke with increasing agitation, and was evidently getting angry.

Mr. Todorovich found himself in an awkward position. He reproached the King for his neglect of the army, and, when challenged to point out wherein consisted his neglect, was unable at a moment's notice to do so. He begged the King to be calm and to remember that when his friends criticised his conduct it was always with the loyal intention to serve his best interests. He reminded the King that somewhere in the Bible it is said that man does not live by bread alone, but by spirit, too. He ought to remember that in his relations with the army. No doubt he took care that his officers got promotion and that their salaries were paid regularly; but between him and his army there was not that *entente* which existed between King Milan and the army. The King of Servia and the Servian Army ought to be one body and one soul. Closeted in his Palace, he communicates with a limited number of higher officers, and the great body of officers are kept at a considerable distance from him. It seems to them that the King has no personal interest in them, and they lose every personal interest in the King. He then mentioned that there were several officers who complained that their lawful rights had been disregarded, that they were badly and unjustly treated. All such things provoke dissatisfaction, and, as a devoted friend of the dynasty, he was alarmed when he heard, positively asserted, that there was serious dissatisfaction with the King in the army.

"Oh, I know well those malcontents in the army!" said the King bitterly." They are mostly younger officers, dissatisfied in consequence of their private interests. But that is nothing extraordinary; it is really inevitable. In the great mass of officers everywhere you will find officers with some failings. In our army there are young officers who were unable to pass successful examinations; there are men who prefer spending their time in playing cards instead of in earnest studies; there are others who were the heroes of all sorts of adventures. Then there are officers who have not been correct in the execution of their official duties, and even some who have been accused, if not convicted, of fraud. Of course, all such men are dissatisfied. But how can I help it? I should have liked, indeed, that all officers were satisfied. But among nearly two thousands officers, is it an extraordinary phenomenon that there are some who are not satisfied? Only, that dissatisfaction has not the meaning which you attribute to it. You exaggerate its importance."

"In such matters it is more advisable to exaggerate the danger than to minimise it," answered Mr. Todorovich. "May God grant that I am wrong. I do not like to disturb your Majesty, and after all it is not my business to submit to you reports about the temper among the officers. But, believe me, Sire, there are certain proceedings in the army which fill me with great anxiety. If you only knew. . . . If you only heard —"

The King interrupted Mr. Todorovich, saying ironically —

"Ah, yes! If I only heard how certain officers abuse myself and the Queen, how they treat us with bad words, and what menaces they utter against us! Do you really think that I do not know it? You are mistaken. I know it in all and in every detail."

"For God's sake, Sire, why then do you treat this state of things with such indifference? Why do you not call all those dissatisfied officers and ask them to tell you frankly what is the matter; talk with them heartily and thoroughly, and when you hear the causes of their dissatisfaction try to remove the same, in order that those officers may see that in you they have not only their Commander-in-Chief, but their friend, their father?"

"How little do you know men!" answered King Alexander. "By acting as you suggest I would only make matters worse. Those men do not understand kindness and generosity. They would interpret it as a proof that I am afraid of them and that I wish to bribe them. But I will find another solution to the difficulty. At present I yet hesitate, simply out of consideration for the public opinion in Europe, that it should not raise the cry: 'Look, there is a conspiracy in the Servian Army!' But if the malcontents continue their agitation, then I will quickly finish my account with them."

He spoke with bitterness and with great decision. He looked gloomy and agitated. He rose up and gave his right hand to his friend. Mr. Todorovich was deeply moved. He bowed over the King's hand and kissed it.

"May God guide you, Sire, in all you do. Try to do it kindly and peaceably. That is the best way."

CHAPTER XV

THE LAST INTERVIEW WITH QUEEN DRAGA

About a year before the catastrophe of 12th June 1903, a friend of King Alexander, Mr. Pera Todorovich, commenced to publish in the serial of his paper, *Male Novine*, a historic novel written by himself, to which he gave the title "A Prophecy," and which had for its foundation the prophecies of the clairvoyant peasant, Mata of Kremna. We refer our readers to the first chapter of this book.

The story had not progressed very far, when King Alexander called Mr. Todorovich to the Palace and asked him to stop the publication. The editor defended himself, as he naturally desired to go on with the story, which had already nearly doubled the circulation of his paper, and which the public bought rapidly and with ever increasing interest.

"You know," said King Alexander, "that we have enemies, you know how they invent and spread all sorts of mischievous stories concerning myself and the Queen. And now you, who are our friend, have found nothing better to do but to write about a prophecy which is believed to forebode nothing pleasant about us."

Mr. Todorovich argued that, after all, it was better that he, a proved friend of the dynasty, should continue the Kremna prophecy in a story ending favourably for the dynasty, than that an enemy of the dynasty should use it against the King. Besides, he had a plot by which everything ended well.

"I do not see how you will be able to end it well, when the prophecy says that my dynasty is to perish. Now, tell me frankly, is not the end of my dynasty foretold? Is it not?"

"Quite so, your Majesty; but I will deal with my story in such a way that everything will be toned down, and end well," said the editor, anxious to continue his very interesting serial.

The King interrupted him rather sharply: "Oh, the devil, you will soften and give it a good end! . . . It would have been far better if you had never started that unfortunate story."

After a few moments of silence, he continued in a somewhat quieter tone —

"After all, as regards myself, I do not care so much for your story; but the Queen is very much annoyed about it. You ought to go to her to explain and excuse yourself. She has a bad opinion of that serial story of yours, and finds fault with you. She spoke to me repeatedly about it. You must go and see her."

Mr. Todorovich did not go at once to see the Queen. He was ill, and engaged otherwise. Several weeks later he was sufficiently well to ask for an audience from the Queen.

She received him standing, and remained so for some time.

"To tell you frankly, Mr. Todorovich," began Queen Draga, "I am angry with you. Formerly I used to read your *Male Novine* with great pleasure and enjoyment; but now, whenever I take a fresh number into my hands, I tremble with fear, lest I find you discoursing on that cursed prophecy!"

Surprised by such an unusual reception, Mr. Todorovich did not know what to say, and was silent. Queen Draga continued —

"For myself personally, I do not care so much. I have hardened my heart against all sorts of annoying stories. But my heart bleeds for the King. He worries about it very much indeed. I am afraid he will be ill. Every day they fill his head with all sorts of reports, so that he gets no sleep. I am afraid the insomnia, from which he has suffered now several months, will in the end kill him."

"For God's sake, your Majesty," Mr. Todorovich said at last, "is it possible that my story in my paper renders the King sleepless?"

"I do not say that exactly; but only that your story disturbs the sleep of the King. But your serial, the rumours and reports, all disagreeable and alarming, conspire together to disturb the King, and to keep him awake. His nerves are so excited that he cannot get even a short nap. How often the dawn finds him fully awake, without having had a moment of sleep. Only when it is full daylight does he get quieter, and falls asleep. But even then his sleep is very disturbed."

"I beg pardon, your Majesty, most humbly," answered Mr. Todorovich. "I had not the slightest idea that my serial could possibly exercise such an impression on the King. His Majesty even told me that he did not care on his own account, but that your Majesty was annoyed about it; and he ordered me to come and explain to you my object, and to apologise if I had done wrong."

"Of course," said the Queen, with a sad smile, "the King will not, either to you, or to anyone, acknowledge that some things do annoy him very much. You remember, for instance, that at the time of his engagement with me, the King was angry with you; but I daresay you do not know why. I will now tell you why. In the number of your paper in which you announced our engagement, and produced our portraits, immediately under them you drew a black mourning line, with several black crosses, and wrote quite a dirge on the death of King Humberto of Italy, his assassination, and his funeral. I thought it was carelessness, and bad taste on your part, to put, immediately below our portraits, the story of an assassination. But with the King the matter was much worse. He hates to hear anything about death. The moment anyone mentions an assassination, or simply death, he changes colour, shivers, and is terribly disturbed, as some persons are when they suddenly see a snake. It is not fear; it is a sort of sickness; it is his nature. I have tried to make him resist this sickly weakness, but so far without success. . . . Of course, I tell you this in confidence, as our faithful and reliable friend."

Thereupon she sat down in an arm-chair, and asked him to take a chair near her.

"Yes," continued the Queen, "because I knew you to be a devoted friend of the King, I have defended you when the King was very angry, believing that you intentionally surrounded our portraits with crosses and a funeral dirge, dealing with death, assassinations, blood, and a catastrophe!"

A conversation followed, concerning the opposition which Mr. Todorovich, and many other friends, made to the King's marriage with Draga. She told him that she knew well his attitude towards her at that time; but she considered him now as not only the King's, but her own friend too.

"Because I consider you to be a faithful and true friend, I tell you the whole truth. The King will never acknowledge to anyone that he is annoyed and disturbed, because it may seem that he is afraid of something. But in truth he is really disturbed and very anxious, and, therefore, the duty of all his friends is to do what they can for his security and for his peace. I am sure you will do so, and, therefore I hope you will stop further publication of 'A Prophecy' in your serial."

"I will do so, your Majesty," answered Mr. Todorovich, "but I cannot understand what there is in the serial so alarming for you."

"Ah! we are not worried at all by what has appeared," said the Queen, quite lively; "but with what is coming ! The King is afraid that the 'Black Prophecy' will be published, and I am annoyed that you write about it, just at the moment when we receive warnings and menaces, and when so many of our enemies wish us all sorts of evil."

"My object in writing the story," said Mr. Todorovich, "was, indeed, to soften what you call '*The Black Prophecy*,' to put it in such a form as would prevent the gloomy impression which it otherwise must produce among the people. I spoke to the King about it."

The Queen asked Mr. Todorovich, would it be possible to tone down the prophecy? She had heard several versions, and would like to hear what Mr. Todorovich knew about it.

Mr. Todorovich asked the Queen if she had read what Mr. Ch. Mijatovich had written about it in the *Male Novine*, as that was the best report as yet published.

"Yes, I have read it," said the Queen; "but Mr. Mijatovich broke off his report at a point when it would have been more interesting to us. He stopped at the ascension of King Alexander to the throne; and we are, of course, more interested to learn what had been foretold concerning us personally; what will happen to us, and what will come after us! Therefore, I should like you to tell me all you know about it. But please do not 'soften' anything, do not hide anything from me. Tell me all."

This is now the story of the Black Prophecy, as told Queen Draga by Mr. Pera Todorovich —

"In the village Kremna, in the district of Ujitza, lived in the last century a man, by name Mata. His village and the neighbourhood considered him somewhat strange, perhaps mentally deranged, although absolutely a quiet and inoffensive man.

"On 28th May, Old Style (9th June, New Style), 1868, he came to the town of Ujitza, as he often used to do. But on that day, in the afternoon, he took up a position in the centre of the principal business street, and called out excitedly —

"'Oh, men! . . . Oh, brethren! For God's sake, help, help! they are killing our ruler. They are killing our Prince! Do not let them! For

God's sake, help! Look, they are slashing him with their yatagans [long Turkish knives]. Oh, oh, look, look! Blood! Oh, how horrible! How terrible! Blood! Blood! Oh, woe to us! . . . Our Prince Michael is murdered!"

Here Queen Draga shuddered visibly.

"Oh, Mr. Todorovich! " she said, "indeed it is terrible. What must that poor man have felt, when, in his madness, he thought he saw that terrible scene?"

Mr. Todorovich continued —

"A great crowd gathered around him, and asked what was the matter, and why he shouted so. He told them that he had just witnessed the assassination of the Prince.

"The police came. They first censured and reproved sharply the 'madman,' for having caused an obstruction in the street, and finally arrested him for 'Having spread false and alarming news about the Sovereign.'

"Next day (29th May, Old Style — 10th June, New Style), in the evening, an official telegram arrived from Belgrade, confirming the assassination of Prince Michael Obrenovich, in the Koshootnyak (the Deer Park), near Belgrade. At first the police suspected that Mata was in the conspiracy, but they soon arrived at the conclusion that it was impossible, and they let him go free.

"While the police had put to him several questions, to elucidate the matter, Mata told them some of his visions, of which several had been already fulfilled; and I believe that others will not be fulfilled if God is the ruler of our destinies and not Satan."

The Queen listened, evidently deeply moved. She was pale, and looked exceedingly sad. With a low and somewhat shaky voice, she said —

"Please, I pray you, continue. What has he told them about future events?"

"Well, your Majesty, the man was later on brought to Belgrade. He was subjected to all sorts of questions at the Home Office, where his statements were put down on paper. King Milan himself had a talk with him. So far as I have been informed, this is what he said: 'Prince Michael will be assassinated, and he will be succeeded by a relative, who will be to a certain extent a torment for the country; he will gain a Royal crown, and under his reign the country will be enlarged and strengthened. He will be a King, but will have many misfortunes. He will die in the prime of life. . . . He will have an only son, who will be still more unfortunate, dying very young, indeed, before his thirtieth year."'

The Queen sighed deeply.

"O God! Is it possible? Before his thirtieth year? Oh, Mr. Todorovich, has the man really said so?"

"Your Majesty has ordered me to tell all and everything, and hide nothing," answered Mr. Todorovich.

"Oh yes. Please go on."

"'He will die young, and with him his candle will be blown out!'"

The Queen interrupted Mr. Todorovich, by asking what he meant by "his candle will be blown out."

"I think," answered Mr. Todorovich, "he meant that the candle which we light and keep burning on the *Saint Patron's days* of our families will burn no longer. In other words, the house of Obrenovich will cease to exist!"

"Terrible!" and the Queen again shuddered, and looked most unhappy. "But please go on."

"'And after his candle shall be blown out, another house will come to reign in Servia. But not for long. Internal struggles and bloodshed, revolts and conflicts will take place, which will cause a foreign army to enter into and occupy Servia. That foreign Power will subject the Servian people to great oppression. There will come such sad and hard times that those who are living, when they pass a churchyard, will say: "Oh, graves, open, that we may lie down and rest. Oh, how happy you are who have died, and are saved from our troubles, misfortunes and shame!" But after many years of great sufferings, a man will appear in the midst of the nation, will raise it up, and lead it against the foreign oppressors; and will succeed in liberating and uniting all the Servians into one and the same free and independent State. Then will commence an epoch of contented and happy life, so much so, that people passing the churchyards will say to those who are dead: "Rise up, dead ones, to see what a happy life we live now."

There Mr. Todorovich stopped his story of the "Black Prophecy." Queen Draga sat in her arm-chair, pale, sad, lost in thought, staring at a point of the soft carpet of the room. It seemed as if she had been turned into a statue.

After some time spent in silence, which her friend dared not interrupt, she raised her head, stared straight at Mr. Todorovich for some time, then, with a deep sigh, she whispered —

"A terrible prophecy! . . . Simply horrible! . . . He will die before his thirtieth year, and he is now in his twenty-seventh year! He has, then, only three years to live! Oh, can it be true?"

She then bent her head low, covered her face with both hands, and apparently wept.

Mr. Todorovich pitied her. Deeply moved and silent, he tried to think of something that could give her some consolation. But he otherwise one of the most intelligent and clever men could not hit upon anything. Then he remembered yet one or two details from the "Black Prophecy."

"Your Majesty, there is yet something that should interest you," he said.

"Yet something?" asked the Queen, raising her head; "what is it?"

"It is this," continued Mr. Todorovich. "The prophet added that the man who will appear in the midst of the people to lead them to liberty and independence, will be in some way a descendant of the Obrenovich Dynasty. He used a figure to explain himself. 'It will be,' he said, 'as if a mighty oak tree has been cut quite near the ground, but after some time, and suddenly from its roots, spreading under the ground, a new branch, at some distance from the original oak, pushes up through the earth, and grows to be a new oak tree.'"

The Queen sadly shook her head.

"Very little consolation for us in that, dear Mr. Todorovich."

Mr. Todorovich continued "It is strange that this extraordinary peasant has foretold not only the increase of Servia's territory, but even the invention of the telephone."

"Indeed!" said the Queen, visibly surprised. "I have not heard that mentioned by anyone."

"Yes, indeed! In his depositions, which have been written down by a secretary, he said among other things: 'The King, sitting in Belgrade, will converse with the Prefects of Ujitza, Negotin, Losnitza, Nish, Pirot, Vranya!' The official, who was writing down his statements, looked at him, surprised, and said: 'Nish, Pirot, Vranya, are not in Servia, but in Turkey!' 'They are now in Turkey, but then they will be in Servia,' answered the peasant. 'And you probably mean the King will communicate with his Prefects by telegraph?' asked the official. 'No, no,' said the prophet; 'not by telegraph, but they, although at great distance, will talk in their own voice, just so as we two talk, and hear each other.' 'That is impossible!' exclaimed the official. 'Now it is impossible; but then it will be quite possible, and the people will be able to talk with each other at great distances.'"

"It is extraordinary," said the Queen. "That detail I have not known. It makes me only more unhappy, because, when this man was able to foretell so exactly the accession of new territories to Servia, and even the invention of the telephone, why, then, should he be wrong on other points? But . . . after all there is one important question: Is it really true that such a man did exist, and that he really said all those things which he is now reported to have said? You know what happens in our days, and in everyday life; someone says only one word, and by the evening he is reported to have said ten."

"That is quite possible, your Majesty," said Mr. Todorovich. "Let us hope that he is not correctly reported, at least in that part concerning the King, and that even if he had been correctly reported his statements concerning the King shall, by God's mercy, not be fulfilled. But concerning the authenticity of his prophecy I have heard that, in the Home Office, or at the Foreign Office, the official acts are kept in two special bundles; and that on one occasion, at the order of the King Milan, they were brought here to the Palace for his perusal."

The Queen said that she would try and get those papers, to see them for herself; but that she must do it without the knowledge of the King, because he would be still more disturbed if he were to read the prophet's statements from the original depositions.

Then, as suddenly she remembered something, she said —

"But, Mr. Todorovich, you never mentioned if there is anything about me personally in that 'Black Prophecy.' Yet some people have told me that there is."

"So far as I know, your Majesty, the clairvoyant of Kremna said only that: 'The King will marry a Servian lady, his own subject, and that she will share with him his destiny.'"

"Oh, my God! What I am praying for is to share with him his destiny! It seems to me the poison would be sweet to me if only I could drink it with him!"

After yet some conversation concerning the possibility of foreseeing events so long a time before they happened, and after his advice that she should order that all the official papers concerning the "Black Prophecy" should be brought to her, Mr. Todorovich took leave from the unhappy Queen.

Neither Queen Draga nor the devoted friend of the dynasty, Mr. Todorovich, had the slightest foreboding that the fulfilment of the "Black Prophecy" was so imminent.

CHAPTER XVI

THE CONSPIRACY

Some fifteen years ago I made the acquaintance of a young and able ex-officer of a great Continental army. I cannot publish his name, but will call him "Count Y." He was very restless, very active, and energetic. He delighted in political intrigue, and was really a born amateur detective. He was a member of several secret societies, and was in touch with the Russian Nihilists, the Bulgarian Committadjis, the Albanian Ligueists, the German Socialists, and the Paris Anarchists.

One of his sweethearts was nothing more than a maid in the service of the Royal family of Italy; another of his sweethearts was a nurse in the Russian Embassy to France, and he corresponded with them. At the same time, in Paris, London, and Vienna, he had access to the best circles of society.

He was quite a psychological and political puzzle, and I became highly interested in him. He had great confidence in me, and often told me things which looked very much like State secrets, or, at least, like secrets of the various secret societies. His stories were not always confirmed by facts, but often they were.

In the summer of the year 1901 he communicated to me in some detail how two of the Great Powers were working to send away King Alexander, and to replace him on the throne by Prince Peter Karageorgevich. I could not believe the story, and did not report it to Belgrade.

In the summer, 1902, he met me by chance in the British Museum, and told me that the agents of a certain Power had approached three influential Servian officers during their cure at Carlsbad that summer, with the suggestion to join in a military *pronunciamento* against King Alexander. The officers refused to enter into the conspiracy, but promised not to allow the soldiers to fire on the people if they should revolt against the King. I reported to King Alexander in a private letter what I had been told, and by whom, advising him at the same time not to attach too much importance to the communication.

In the autumn of 1902 that gentleman made a special appointment to meet me in town (he lived then out of town), and communicated to me that certain papers had been exchanged between a certain pretender and a certain Great Power, and that, according to his information, the doom of King Alexander was sealed. I personally could hardly believe it; but I still considered it my duty to make a report to King Alexander.

In the very beginning of 1903 my informant came to the Servian Legation to tell me that one of the plans (there being several plans) of the conspirators was to organise a public meeting, so that the crowd would go *en masse* apparently with loyal intentions past the Palace, then rush into the Palace, overwhelm the guards, and assassinate King Alexander. Again I communicated to the King what I had heard, advising him to take precautionary measures, although this particular communication might not have any real foundation.

In the light of subsequent events, my informant was evidently far better informed than I could have ever credited him.

In the light of those events, certain impressions which I received in Vienna in the first days of January 1902, had quite a peculiar significance. Travelling from Belgrade to the Tyrol, I stopped a few days in Vienna, and saw some of the most influential personages of the Austrian political circles. I was not surprised to learn that they had been disgusted by the conduct of King Alexander on the question of his marriage. But I was struck by certain impressions, which led me to suspect that the question of replacing King Alexander by Prince Peter Karageorgevich was completely arranged between Russia and Austria. I was plainly told that Austria could never more believe the word of Alexander, and that if the Servians were to choose Peter Karageorgevich to-morrow for their King, or anyone else, excepting the Prince of Montenegro, Austria would acknowledge the free choice of the Servian people. Of course, I do not mean to insinuate that Austria and Russia knew, and much less that they approved, the methods by which the Servian conspirators proposed to make the change on the Servian throne. But already, towards the end of 1901, they must have come to an understanding concerning the possible, or even probable, change on the throne of Servia.

Queen Draga, in the last interview which Mr. Todorovich had with her, not many days before her assassination, told the King's friend that both she and the King had received for some time information that a conspiracy against them was in preparation, and that many officers, especially young ones, had entered into it. Some of these communications were made by anonymous letters, others confidentially in a personal interview. Some of the informers asserted that the conspiracy had been organised and was directed from abroad, others that it had started spontaneously with a certain group of officers. The Queen had the impression that the conspiracy was organised by someone outside Servia, who seemed to be an experienced conspirator. To the young officers drawn into the conspiracy it had been cleverly suggested that they would act as patriots and heroes if they were to deliver the country from such an unworthy King and Queen.

It seems the conspiracy was definitely organised shortly after the return of Colonel Mashin from Russia, in the autumn of 1902. The Colonel placed himself at its head, taking as his principal coadjutors Lieutenant-Colonel Damyan Popovich and Lieutenant-Colonel Mishich. These three superior officers were in secret communication with another body, composed of civilians, enemies for personal reasons of Alexander and Draga, or inveterate enemies of the Obrenovich Dynasty, like Lyuba Zivkovich, Stoyan Protich, Atza Stanoyevich, Nicola Hadji-Thoma. At the head of this civilian body of conspirators was Mr. Genchich, formerly the Home Minister of King Alexander, but who, after the marriage of the King with Draga, was condemned, for an open letter to the King, in which he criticised his conduct, to seven years' imprisonment, although he was released in the second year of his confinement. Their object was not only to annihilate the Obrenovich Dynasty, but to put on the throne the Karageorgevich Dynasty.

Once decided to murder King Alexander and Queen Draga, the only question that remained was when and where to do it.

I do not know if the incidents of the 6th (19th) March 1903 had anything to do with the attempt to kill the Royal couple. A meeting of shop assistants and students was arranged to take place, to protest against certain police measures concerning shop assistants. Somebody suggested that the whole meeting should proceed to pass the Royal

Palace. A great crowd moved through the principal streets towards the Palace. But thirty yards from the Palace the crowd was stopped by the police, and when it refused to disperse was fired on! According to the official reports only a few people were killed and wounded. The opposition papers again exaggerated the number. I say I do not know if those incidents have not been a cover for a planned attack on the Palace and the Royal couple. They looked, in some respects at least, very much like the plan which was communicated to me by Count Y. only two months before.

But there seems to be no doubt that Palm Sunday, 6th (19th) April, was really selected for the execution of the murderous attack on the Royal couple. Under the reign of the Obrenovichs Palm Sunday was a national fete day, in commemoration of the second and successful rising of the Servians under Milosh Obrenovich against the Turks. To the church ceremony in the Cathedral in Belgrade was added, since 1868, a short religious and military ceremony in the Citadel of Belgrade, in commemoration of the delivery of that fortress by the Turks to Prince Michael Obrenovich on the Palm Sunday of 1867. In the Citadel a kiosk was raised, in which every year a *Te Deum* was sung in the presence of the King, State dignitaries, officers, citizens, and a part of the Belgrade garrison. According to what the Queen told Mr. Todorovich, a day or two before Palm Sunday the King received information that fifteen young officers had sworn to surround him on that day in the kiosk in the fortress, and to cut him and the Queen to pieces with their swords. The kiosk would have to be surrounded on all four sides by the soldiers under the command of officers taking part in the conspiracy. In consequence of this information the King and Queen did not go either to the Cathedral or to the fortress. As it happened to be raining that day, the official and semi-official papers explained that the Royal couple could not attend the Palm Sunday celebration on account of the bad weather.

Shortly afterwards the foundation stone of the Home of Arts in Belgrade was to be laid, and the King and the Queen were to perform the ceremony, to which they both looked forward with pleasure. But they received, just in time, a communication that certain officers had decided to murder them! The communication came from a man who received full credence. The King and the Queen at the last moment gave up going to the ceremony, and in that way frustrated the second plan of the conspirators.

The Queen told Mr. Todorovich that the conspirators intended to murder them one evening while they were in the circus; but at the last moment they gave the intention up, finding that very many gendarmes were placed around the circus who would fire on them, and, as the circus was always full, many innocent people would be sacrificed.

Adjoining the southern carriage road, by which the carriages generally leave the Palace, is a large building, of which the first ground floor is occupied by the Home Office, and the first floor by the Foreign Office. The principal salon of the latter has a balcony, which is walled in, but cut at short intervals, just as if it was prepared for fighting, or firing down on the principal, but comparatively narrow, road. The King and the Queen cannot go out or drive from the Palace without passing that building. The conspirators thought that the balcony of the Foreign Office formed an excellent ambush, from which to fire on the King and the Queen. Four of them had been selected by lot. A servant of the Foreign Office was approached with a heavy bribe, to take in secretly their rifles, and allow them to hide themselves on the balcony. But again one of the conspirators had pity on the young King, and sent him information anonymously. The leaders of the conspiracy were, on the other hand, informed by someone in the Palace that suspicious orders had been given to the police to watch the balcony. They at once recognised that the plan was betrayed, and gave it up.

It was evident not only that a conspiracy was in permanent existence, but that the conspirators were determined to murder the King and Queen. Since the beginning of the year 1903 they lived like two persons condemned to death, expecting every moment to see the executioners enter their cells. They had no peace, no rest; they were in a permanent nervous excitement, which ended by a general prostration. Never in the history of the world have a King and Queen undergone more terrible penalty; during, at least, the last five months of their life, they suffered as if they had been stretched and tortured on a rack.

When Queen Draga confided all this suffering to the faithful and sympathetic Todorovich, this friend of the dynasty exclaimed —

"But if all those informations which the King received were true, then the situation is simply horrible!"

"Of course it is horrible!" said the Queen. "But there is something that wears us and exhausts our strength more than the danger — it is the uncertainty. You just said yourself, 'If all those informations were true!' That is just what torments the King more than anything else. We have asked ourselves all these months: 'Can it be true? Is it possible that the Servian officers thirst for the blood of their King and Queen?' This uncertainty paralyses the King's usual energy and decisiveness, and cripples his action. When we consult our devoted friends about it, we find that everyone has some special opinion of the matter. Some friends come and exclaim in great alarm: 'For God's sake, why are you waiting? Do you not see that you are in imminent danger of your lives?' A few days since a friend came to tell us how, in the circle of the conspirators, someone drew attention to the fact that of late the King hardly ever left the Palace, whereupon some of them remarked: 'Yes, the bear has withdrawn into his cave; but we will go and find him there. . . .' We had such a case as this. A young officer came and insisted to see the King privately. Admitted into the King's presence, he, in the greatest agitation, trembling and shaking, confessed that he was one of the conspirators, that he had given his word of honour to his comrades not to separate himself from them; but, overwhelmed with irresistible pity for the youth of the King, he came to implore him to try to save himself. But then, General Milovan (the Minister of War), and General Tzintzar-Markovich (the Premier), characterised the story of the young officer as an invention, as a speculation to get promotion, and such like. They were sure that the young man had not understood what his superior officer had told him. They even suggested that he ought to be punished for spreading false news, and alarming the King. Especially General Tzintzar-Markovich — and he ought to know — assured the King that it is simply impossible that any officer conspired against the King.

I do not wish to mention any names. But to show you what confusion prevails in the Palace and around us, I will tell you one thing. You know that Lieutenant-Colonel Mika Naoumovich is among all the equerries at the Court the greatest favourite of the King. If the King could take off his own head, he would trust it to the keeping of his faithful Mika. You know probably that Mika and Boza (the Prefect of the Police) are chums and bosom friends. Well, Boza told the King that he had reasons to suspect the loyalty of his friend Mika, and implored the King to send him away from the Palace. But the first Aide-de-Camp, General Laza, and the Premier, General Tzintzar-Markovich, laughed at the suspicion as simply ludicrous. Now, what is the poor King to do, when his most trusted friends give him totally opposite advice?

"Yes," continued the Queen; "some of our best friends come to the King and say: 'Why are you waiting? Do you not see clearly the nest of the conspiring snakes?' The moment the King prepares to act, other not less faithful and trusted friends rush in: 'For God's sake, Sire, don't! You will strike innocent men, and then you will provoke a terrible misfortune.' Some cry: 'Don't wait!' Others again: 'Do wait!' The King gets perplexed. One day he follows the advice of one group of friends, and several suspected officers have been arrested. The next day he listens to the other group, and then orders the release of the arrested officers. Such a procedure has spoilt everything, and taught the conspirators to be more careful. The faithful and loyal officers are now systematically avoided by the conspirators, and they themselves (the loyal officers), having seen that by their loyalty to their King they have only succeeded in compromising themselves with their comrades, find it better to be silent. As I mentioned, this uncertainty, this confusion, this perplexity, is quite a curse to us. It prevents the King having rest and sleep.

"The King himself," continued the Queen, "is sometimes cheerful; but of late that is less and less frequent. There are days and nights in which he is overwhelmed by sadness, anxiety, and something like fear. Some nights he sits in his working room the whole night, lost in deep thought. I go to him, and try to cheer him up, and to induce him to go to bed. But it is no use. Often, in the morning, I find him sitting, fully dressed, in his arm-chair. Sometimes he comes to my bedroom, draws a chair near the bed, takes my hand in his, and sits pale and silent for a long time. One night he came to me just when I was beginning to doze. He took my hand in his, kissed it, and said with a very, very sad voice: 'Queen of Servia, whom hatest thou?' 'What do you mean, Sasha?' 'Whom hatest thou, Queen of Servia?' 'Oh, my dear Sasha, what is the matter with you? Why should I hate anyone? I do not hate anyone!' 'Nor do I hate anyone. And yet we are hated! And hated just by those to whom we have done so many kindnesses. And why do they hate me? Is it because I am the son of a King, and King myself, and not the son of a fisherman, born in a hut somewhere on the Danube? But if my Kingship is my crime, what have you done to them, you a weak woman?' He was pale, his hands were cold as ice, and tears were rolling down his face."

This was the last interview of Queen Draga with a journalist, who was, at the same time, an intimate friend.

CHAPTER XVII

THE ASSASSINATION

June 10th, 1903, was a sunny and a very sultry day in Belgrade.

A distinguished friend of mine went, about 11 o'clock in the morning, to the Palace to see the King. At that hour a company of King's Own Guardsmen — all picked and handsome young men — under the command of Captain Panayotovich, was marching with drums and bugles into the Courtyard of the Old Palace, to replace a company of infantry which was doing the duties of the Palace guard since the previous day.

Captain Panayotovich had the reputation of an excellent and brave officer, devoted with absolute loyalty to his duty and to his King.

My friend went to the waiting-room of the Old Palace. The equerry doing duty on that day was Lieutenant-Colonel Michael (otherwise called Mika) Naoumovich. His father was well known as a devoted partisan of Karageorgevich, but Lieutenant-Colonel Michael Naoumovich was considered as entirely devoted to the Obrenovich Dynasty. King Milan patronised him very much, and King Alexander not only took him for one of his equerries, but repeatedly saved him from awkward situations, and paid his debts. Only a few days before, King Alexander gave him 20,000 dinars (£800) to pay off his latest debts. As an officer he was reputed to be an able commander; but as a man he was of dissolute habits, a gambler and heavy drinker. At that very moment he was a traitor to his King and benefactor. When my friend entered the small waiting-room he found Naoumovich's big and heavy form seemingly quite collapsed in an arm-chair.

He rose up slowly, with evident effort, to greet my friend. He was quite yellow, evidently depressed, and in bad spirits. In violation of the regulations, he came unshaved that day to his duty in the

Palace. My friend thought he looked as if he had spent the previous night in debauchery, and had left home without washing his face. He seemed somewhat dazed and troubled. "What is the matter with you, Colonel?" asked my friend.

"I am ill, very ill," he answered. "I am suffering from a fever, which I am trying to drive away by strong cognac. Shall we take a glass together?"

He knew what was going to happen that night. He knew that that was to be the last day of the King, who had been always kind to him, to whom he had sworn to be faithful, and whom he now was on the point to betray. He did not know that that was to be also his own last day. But God knows what forebodings he might have had that very morning, when my friend saw him physically so collapsed!

A few moments later, the first Aide-de-Camp to the King, General Laza Petrovich, entered. General Petrovich was one of the handsomest and smartest officers of the Servian Army. He was nicknamed "Lepi Laza," the "Handsome Laza." Looking very smart in the Servian General's uniform, well-groomed, as if he had been an English officer, a pleasant smile in his dark eyes, and always ready to laugh and show his fine teeth, he came in to greet heartily my friend, and to joke with him. He seemed quite happy. Evidently he had no foreboding that in about twelve hours he would witness a terrible massacre, and be dead himself.

King Alexander received my friend for a few minutes only. He was in the Servian General's undress uniform. He looked well, and seemed to be in good spirits. He explained to my friend that he could not talk with him then, as he had invited the Austro-Hungarian Military Attaché to an interview, and Colonel Pomyankovsky was waiting in the drawing-room for an audience. He asked my friend to come to the Palace that evening, "when they would have plenty of time to talk together."

Poor King Alexander, poor young man! Little did he think that his time was very short indeed, that he was living then the last hours of his life, and that in less than twelve hours he would be cruelly assassinated!

That afternoon was unusually hot and sultry for the time of the year. As if it had been the middle of summer, everybody remained indoors, and only towards the evening came out for a walk on the "Teraziya" — the principal street on the ridge of the triangular elevation on which Belgrade is built, and which, passing the Palace, leads on to the Citadel's glacier, transformed into a pretty park. Owing to the sultriness of the air people expected a great storm that night.

At seven o'clock in the evening, in the small waiting-room of the Old Palace were to be seen the smart and smiling "Handsome Laza," who was positively cheerful; the unshaven and evidently deeply agitated Lieutenant-Colonel Naoumovich, who looked then even worse than at noon of that day; the Home Minister, Mr. Velya Todorovich, who seemed to be in a cheerful mood, as if the secret police had not informed him that a conspiracy might explode any day, and at any time; the handsome, elegant, and certainly very able Mr. Lyuba Novakovich, Minister of Agriculture, Commerce, and Industry; and the spare figure and pale face of Mr. Zivan Zivanovich, the Minister of Public Instruction. That face looked somewhat colder and sterner than usual. Mr. Zivanovich is generally believed to have known not only that a military conspiracy was in existence, but, also, that that very night something would be attempted against the King! With them in the waiting-room was also the Servian Minister to Bulgaria, Mr. Paul Marinkovich, whom the young King wished specially to see that night.

A few minutes later an equerry entered the room, to inform the Cabinet Ministers of the King's desire to see them at once, and all three together. Mr. Marinkovich was called to the Queen.

What the King said to his Ministers, I do not know.

Mr. Marinkovich was kind enough to inform me of the subject of Queen Draga's conversation with him.

The Queen looked sadly depressed. He thought she received him coldly. I should say she, with a woman's sensitiveness and intuition, felt vaguely the approaching danger. She complained of the situation, which she described as "simply awful."

"We know that something is going on against us; we know that Russia is working against the King; this is a terrible evil, and all our friends ought to stand by us, and help us!"

This conversation was interrupted by the arrival of the Premier, General Tzintzar-Markovich. I believe he was sent for by the Queen. Mr. Marinkovich rose and left them. He was immediately called to the King. It was exactly 7.45 p.m.

King Alexander kept his envoy to Bulgaria nearly two and a half hours. They discussed a very confidential and very important subject.

About the Christmas of 1902, King Alexander decided to enter into an alliance with Bulgaria, and declare war on Turkey. Mr.

Marinkovich was entrusted with the negotiations of a secret Treaty with Bulgaria. Meantime the Servian General Staff had elaborated all the details of the invasion of the Kossovo Vilayet by the Servian Army. Alexander gave all his energetic interest to this great subject. He discussed — only a few hours before his officers arrived to murder him — with his Minister to Bulgaria all the diplomatic details, and the great features of the military plans for the liberation of "Old Servia" and Macedonia. This circumstance only deepens the tragic elements in this great tragedy.

The King told his envoy that the War Minister, General Milovan Pavlovich, was of opinion that action should not begin before September of that year; but that by that time the Servian Army would be ready to take the field.

The last note which King Alexander made with his own hand that fateful night, ran as follows: —

"To order the Finance Minister to insure the regular payment of salaries to the officers and the men of the Pirot garrison, and tell the War Minister to issue orders to the commander of that garrison to instruct his officers to go as often as possible across the frontier to meet the Bulgarian officers, and to fraternise with them; and for that object the officers to receive more frequently extra pocket-money."

At 10.30 p.m., General Tzintzar-Markovich entered the room, in which King Alexander was absorbed in talking, with his Bulgarian Envoy, of the prepared plans for the Serbo-Bulgarian action against the Turks.

"For Heaven's sake, Sire," said the Premier, "have pity on this young man! The Queen is very angry with him, thinking that because of him you keep her waiting for the supper all this time."

The King rose at once, and all three proceeded to the large entrance hall, leading to the Queen's room and to the dining-room. On their way there, the King said to his Premier —

"Mito,[1] the Bulgarian[2] says that he believes the thing would be quite possible. But as it is now already so late, you had both better come to-morrow to dine with me, and after dinner we will discuss all the points!'

---

1 Diminutive from Demeter, which was the Christian name of General Tzintzar-Markovich.
2 King Alexander called by that nickname Mr. Markinovich.

In the entrance hall, in a corner, the musicians of the Guards were waiting to commence to play during supper. A little farther, Captain Nikodiye Lunyevitza, the Queen's younger brother, was standing with a few officers. There was also the equerry on duty, Lieutenant-Colonel Naoumovich, in full uniform. He looked very ill.

"Naoum! what is the matter with you? You look so unwell!" said the King to him.

"I am ill, your Majesty!" answered the traitor with trembling voice.

"Why have you then not asked to be relieved of duty to-night?" asked poor King Alexander sympathetically; but without waiting for the answer, he hurried to the Queen's boudoir, to fetch her to the supper.

At that hour in the guard-house in the courtyard of the Palace strange doings were in progress. Naoumovich had sent to the officers' room the strongest wines which the King's cellar could supply.

Second Lieutenant of the Guards, Peter Zivkovich, was pouring glass after glass to the loyal commander Captain P. Panayotovich. It is believed that Zivkovich, who was in the conspiracy, drugged the wine which he served to the Commander of the Guards. Before the King and Queen retired, about midnight, to their rooms, their faithful Commander of the Guards was in a deep sleep, lying absolutely unconscious on a sofa in the officers' room of the Guards.

After a hot and sultry day, the coffee-houses and "beer-gardens" of Belgrade were filled with people. Especially the garden of the well-known Restaurant "Kolaratz," opposite the National Theatre, and about half-way between the fortress and the Palace, was very full. At one table sat Lieutenant-Colonel Peter Mishich, his dark face looking very serious, while he talked in low tones to a younger man in civilian dress. That man was his own brother-in-law, Dushan Vouich, who was soon to assume the duties of the Prefect of the Police. Not far from his table, about ten younger officers were sitting together, smoking and drinking beer. A group of officers were drinking in the little garden in front of the hotel "The Servian Crown," almost opposite the principal entrance to the fortress. They seemed to be much excited. They repeatedly ordered the gipsy musicians to play the March of Queen Draga. They were drinking heavily. Other conspirators were gathered in the Officers' Club, not quite two thousand yards from the Palace. They were also drinking, and seemed more than usually hilarious.

Alexander Mashin, colonel on the retired list, the organiser of the plot, and the chief of the executive committee of the conspirators, was that evening on a visit to his friend Colonel Yovan Pavlovich, once Treasurer of the King, but now placed on the retired list because he disapproved of the King's marriage with Draga Mashin. Colonel Mashin's parents were of the Czek nationality, and emigrated to Servia from Bohemia during the reign of Prince Alexander Karageorgevich. His father was a very able physician, and was one of the Court doctors to Prince Karageorgevich, and remained faithful to that dynasty to the end of his days. But as Alexander Mashin showed great intelligence, and was a promising young officer, King Milan took him under his own special protection, made him one of his aides-de-camp, and by his influence decided his son Alexander to send Mashin as Envoy Extraordinary and Minister Plenipotentiary to Montenegro, and in 1899 as Servia's Military Expert Delegate to the International Peace Conference at the Hague. It was well known that, for reasons unexplained, Colonel Mashin hated his sister-in-law Draga, the widow of his elder brother Svetozar Mashin, and that his hatred was intensified after her marriage with King Alexander.

I do not know what was the subject of conversation between the two Colonels, both of whom were placed on the retired list because of Draga. Probably they spoke of the common subject of their hatred. But Colonel Yovan Pavlovich knew nothing about the conspiracy.

After 11 o'clock p.m., Mashin often looked at his watch to see the time. It seemed as if he had an appointment which he was anxious not to miss.

At about a quarter to twelve he left his friend; but half an hour later he reappeared in Colonel Pavlovich's house. This time he was dressed in the full uniform of a Colonel of the standing army, and his astonished friend asked him what it all meant. Mashin told him everything was arranged to liberate, that very night, the Servian people of Alexander and his Draga, and of the Obrenovichs altogether, and call Peter Karageorgevich to the throne. Colonel Pavlovich was greatly shocked. He implored Mashin to desist from the decision to assassinate Alexander and Draga.

"It is now too late! The thing must be done! But as I may be killed this night myself, here is my last will and testament, and I leave my wife and children to your friendship," answered Colonel Mashin, and hurried away.

He went straight to the Palilula Barracks, where King Alexander's own Vllth Regiment of Infantry was quartered. The commander of the first battalion of that regiment, Major Milivoy Angyelkovich, received him and introduced him as the new Commander of the Danubian Division (to which the regiment belonged), whose orders implicitly to obey King Alexander had specially commanded them. Colonel Mashin ordered the entire regiment under arms at once. Some detachments were entrusted to certain officers, who started immediately for their destination. The remainder of the regiment was led by the Colonel towards the Palace, and surrounded it on the northern, eastern, and southern sides. They reached the Palace somewhat later than arranged, and for a quarter of an hour Mishich and other officers, who were already in front of the Palace, had misgivings that something was wrong.

Colonel Mishich, leaving the Kolaratz garden, went to the fortress, and brought out the VIth Infantry Regiment, which he had placed in the comparatively narrow street between the Russian Legation and the small front garden of the Old Palace.

The Police Commissioner, seeing the troops emerging at midnight from the fortress, and moving in the direction of the Palace, telephoned to the Prefect of Police, Marshityanin, whom he knew to be at home. This gentleman, undoubtedly devoted to the King, and generally considered a sharp-witted official, lost his wits, and, instead of telephoning the report to the Palace, he peevishly ordered the Commissioner to address the officer doing duty at the Central Police Station. The officer on duty at that station for that night was a young man, brother-in-law of the King's first Aide-de-Camp, General Petrovich. Instead of spending the night at the station, he went to enjoy himself with some friends, leaving in his place a young clerk, who did not know what to do when someone telephoned that troops were moving towards the Palace. If these two small misadventures had not happened, if the King had been advised of the movements of the troops in time, he might have taken the command of his Guards, and of the gendarmerie in the adjacent courtyard, telephoned to the barracks, and to the Banyitza Camp for help; and events might have taken another turn. But fatality decided that it should be otherwise.

At about half-past twelve the troops had surrounded the Palace. None of the soldiers knew what was going on. Some of the officers who were with the troops did not know either. They were told confidentially, by the officers who were in the conspiracy, that the

King had decided to send away Queen Draga, and that he had ordered the troops to come to the Palace to assist him without disturbing the order and peace of the town.

About twenty officers appeared at that moment before the southern iron gate, leading from the street to the courtyard of the Palace.

One of them gave by whistle a signal.

Second Lieutenant Zivkovich, having caused his commander, Captain Panayotovich, to fall into a deep sleep, took the keys of the gates. Hearing the whistle signal, he hurried to the southern gate, opened it, and let in the officers who were impatiently waiting there.

As they rushed up the paved carriage drive, they made sufficient noise to alarm a sergeant of the Guards, who, seeing at the same time a crowd, shouted to the Guards: "To arms! To arms!"

The soldiers ran out of their rooms and grasped their rifles. One of the inrushing officers fired his revolver at the loyal sergeant, and killed him on the spot.

Second Lieutenant Zivkovich, Commander of the company of the Guards on duty, sprang forward, drew his sword, and cried to his men: "Stand still!"

In a few seconds the company was standing at attention.

Zivkovich addressed them —

"The King's orders are that you do not move from here whatever takes place around you!" He stood in front, to prevent them moving.

Some of the conspirators rushed to the rooms of the first Aide-de-Camp of the King, General Petrovich, who seemed not yet to have gone to bed. He rushed out, dressed, to see what was the matter, when he heard the shot which killed the sergeant, and was met by the conspirators, of whom one fired at him, wounding him on the left arm. Others seemed to disapprove, and left one or two of their comrades to bandage the wound of the General, and to keep watch over him.

The crowd of officers then rushed to the entrance door of the Old Palace. It was to have been opened to them by the King's equerry, Lieutenant-Colonel Naoumovich, but in consequence of the agitation of the whole day, and possibly owing to continuous heavy drinking, he had fallen into a heavy sleep, and did not hear his co-conspirators at the door of the Palace. His comrades had to break the door open with a dynamite cartridge. Its terrible detonation was heard all over the town, exactly at half-past twelve, awakening many people, and bringing them out of their houses into the street to discover what was the matter. The detonation, and the shaking of the building, awakened Naoumovich, who then hurried to meet his comrades. But they were so enraged with him for his dangerous negligence, or his treachery, that one of them, by name Captain Dragutin Dimitriyevich, shot him dead on the spot. It is an extraordinary circumstance that the officer who killed Naoumovich was, according to general rumour in Belgrade, the lover of Naoumovich's wife! Another version is that Naoumovich, who was waiting and watching, fully dressed, for the arrival of his co-conspirators, did open the outside door of the building to them, and smashed the door of the great *salon* by a dynamite cartridge; but, agitated as he was, he bungled over it, and was himself killed by the explosion.

Anyhow, the conspirators obtained access to the inner rooms of the Palace at a few minutes after half-past twelve.

Meanwhile the dynamite explosion at the Palace, in addition to revolver shots which were heard, opened the eyes of the gendarmes in the next courtyard to the Palace courtyard, and they began to fire on the crowd which they saw in the Palace yard, and in front of the Palace door.

Not quite five hundred yards from the Palace was the police station for that part of the town, which is called "Teraziya." The gendarmes of that station, about ten or fifteen men, hearing the explosion in the Palace, and seeing what seemed to be a crowd of people in the street in front of the Old Palace, began to fire on them. But that apparent crowd were soldiers of the VIth Regiment, who answered by firing their rifles at the police station, and for ten minutes or a quarter of an hour it seemed as if a battle were raging around the Palace.

But at the order of Lieutenant-Colonel Mishich, a detachment of the VIth Regiment succeeded in mastering the few gendarmes of the police station, having killed some of them. The gendarmes of the Palace, in the courtyard next to the Palace courtyard, were stopped firing by the Commander of the Infantry Guards, Captain Luba Kostich, who arrived there with the whole regiment of the Guards, and told them that what was going on had been ordered by the King, who wanted to send away Queen Draga.

The explosion of the dynamite cartridge had broken the electric light wires. There was perfect darkness in the Palace. The officers, led by Captain Dragutin Dimitriyevich, who, in consequence of his strength and brutality, was nicknamed "Apis," and who already had killed Naoumovich and a soldier of the sentry, were groping through the rooms, shouting terrible menaces, and blaspheming in a horrible manner. With great difficulty they forced one or two servants to get them a few candles. They sent one of their own comrades across the street to Dr. Gashich's house to get some. By the help of these candles they searched every corner of the Palace, looking under every sofa and behind every curtain, striking the walls with their swords to detect any secret door in them. But there was no trace anywhere of the Royal couple. Yet their bed seemed to have been occupied, and a French book was on a small table near the bed, lying open, as if it had just been thrown there in haste.

They ordered the wounded General Petrovich to be brought in. He was brought in, two conspirators holding his arms. They told him that they would spare his life if he told them where the King and Queen were hiding. He assured them that he had no idea where they were. They began to strike him with their swords, shouting, in their rage, insults and disgusting oaths. He maintained that he did not know. At last he said —

"You have not been to the New Palace, perhaps they are there!"

They had been searching the rooms of the Old Palace nearly a whole hour. They thought their search was really thorough. They therefore, after a short consultation, decided to go to the New Palace, which is not quite two hundred yards from the old one, and in the same courtyard. They all left the Old Palace.

On crossing the threshold into the open air, poor General Petrovich said —

"Gentlemen, you have hats on your heads, I am bareheaded. As I have not much hair, and there is a cool breeze, I may catch cold. Please send someone to fetch me my hat."

A young lieutenant put his own cap on the General's head.

In the courtyard, Colonels Mashin, Solarovich, Atanaskovich, Lieutenant-Colonel Mishich, and a few other officers, were standing opposite the entrance door of the Old Palace. They were astonished to see the crowd of officers coming out.

Colonel Mashin stepped quickly forward, and asked the excited crowd of younger officers —

"What on earth are you doing? Where are you going?"

"They are nowhere to be found in this old house," some of them answered; "and General Laza said it may be that they are gone to the New Palace, and we are leading him there to show us the rooms."

"You fools!" shouted Mashin in a rage. "Do you not see that this rogue" (he actually used a few indecent words) "is only making dupes of you to gain time? Back at once to the Palace, and we will go with you!"

And they all — Mashin, Mishich, Solarovich, Atanaskovich, and the others — returned to the Old Palace on a new search.

Meanwhile King Alexander and Queen Draga were hidden in the small alcove, to which they had access through a secret door in the papered walls of the bedroom. The iron door fitted so closely in the wall that in the broad daylight it could hardly be discovered. What those two poor people thought and said to each other while they listened to the firing in the yard and in the Palace, and to the shouts of the infuriated, half-drunken officers in search after them, God only knows! They certainly must have known that it was imminent and violent death which was in search of them. They must have heard the shocking curses, disgusting oaths, and the terrible menaces, which those wild beasts in human form had been uttering during their apparently useless search of nearly two hours. The deeper their devotion to each other, the greater their ambition to do great and splendid deeds as King and Queen, the more intense must have been their mental suffering and agony before the bullets from the revolvers and the sharp swords of their officers reached their trembling bodies. The agony of their souls, lasting for nearly two hours, I imagine must have caused them far greater sufferings than the physical agony of their mutilated, massacred, dying bodies. The poor young man, the poor woman ambitious to wear the Royal crown, have paid a tremendous price for their ambitions, for their follies and sins. I am sure not one of my readers will ever wish for a moment, even his or her bitterest and most hated enemy, to suffer, for five minutes, what King Alexander and Queen Draga had suffered for nearly two hours!

Did they pray to God in those terrible moments? Alexander did not believe in God, but Draga did. I daresay she prayed more fervently than she ever prayed in her life. They certainly both wanted to be saved. That intense desire to be saved brought about quicker their horrible end.

The alcove in which they remained hidden had a window facing the front of the Palace, and the narrow street lined with horse-chestnut trees, in which lived the Tzar's Envoy Extraordinary and Minister Plenipotentiary, Mr. Tcharikoff, who was actually at one of his windows, watching, no doubt in great agitation, the development of the tragedy of which he was confidentially informed three or four days before.

Queen Draga was leaning her forehead against the window, and peering into the semi-obscurity towards the Russian Legation, probably in the hope that every moment the doors of the Legation would open, and the Tzar's Minister step forward to claim, in his master's name, the lives of those two unhappy people, whose marriage he, as the principal witness, endorsed before the Servians and before the world at large. But no! He was at the window, looking, perhaps, not without pity; but seemingly helpless!

The poor Queen Draga noticed in the garden an officer walking slowly among the bushes. She peered more intently, and piercing the obscurity of a June night, she recognised the Commander of the Royal Guard, Captain Luba Kostich. Surely the Royal Guards will be faithful to their oath; surely the Commander of the Royal Guards will be loyal to his King! Poor Queen Draga hastily opened the window, and shouted in evident distress, and at the top of her voice —

"Soldiers! Your King is in danger! For God's sake, to the rescue, to the rescue!"

The Commander of the faithful Guards stopped pacing the flower garden. He recognised the Queen's voice, saw her distinctly, and fired his revolver at her! She hastily drew the blinds. It was too late.

Captain Kostich ran up the staircase to the first floor, to the still bewildered and enraged conspirators, and told them where the King and Queen were hiding, as he had seen the Queen at the window of the alcove.

Still they did not discover the door leading to the alcove. They called for an axe. An axe was speedily brought from the woodshed in the courtyard. Lieutenant — began to strike the wall with it.

General Petrovich saw that in a few seconds the axe would strike the door, behind which he knew the King and the Queen were standing. Trembling and pale, from emotion more than from pain and loss of blood from his wound, he said —

"Gentlemen, will you give me your word of honour that you will spare the life of the King?"

Several voices in the excited crowd answered, "Yes."

General Petrovich turned to a certain point of the papered wall and knocked.

"Sire! Sire!" he shouted. "Open! Open! I am your Laza. Here are your officers!"

The door opened slowly.

There stood King Alexander and Queen Draga, both of them hastily and insufficiently dressed, as they had sprung from their bed. They found themselves facing a dense group of officers.

It was a historic but terrible tableau!

King Alexander stepped forward in front of the Queen, as if to shelter her, looked straight at the traitors, and said —

"What is it you want? . . . And what of your oath of fidelity to me?"

There was a second or two of deadly silence. They looked at each other as if mesmerised.

Then Lieutenant —, who before entering the army was a teacher in a village school, cried out —

"What are you standing gazing at? Here is our oath of fidelity to him!!!"

Saying this, he fired on the King, who sank into the arms of Draga.

In a moment several revolvers were fired on the falling King and on the Queen. They both then dropped on the floor. The enraged conspirators continued for a few seconds firing their revolvers at the Royal couple, bleeding and groaning on the floor. They then drew their swords, and began to slash them in all directions. The poor woman, Queen Draga, was especially the object of their revolting cruelty.

I cannot describe the horrible, disgusting, and ferocious conduct of some of those murderers. They seemed to emulate the exploits of Jack-the-Ripper on the dead body of the woman who was their Queen. As I write these lines, I feel utter shame and humiliation that Servian officers could have conducted themselves with such brutal cruelty!

Fortunately the poor woman was killed instantly by the first volley aimed at her.

King Alexander, although pierced by several bullets, was not dead. He groaned in agony, in a pool of blood. It is not certain that he was conscious.

Lieutenant-Colonel Mishich suggested that the bodies of the King and Queen should be thrown out of the window, into the flower garden, that the soldiers surrounding the Palace should see that they were dead.

He opened the window. Bending over it he shouted —

"Long live Peter Karageorgevich, King of Servia!"

The officers in front of their soldiers echoed his cry by shouting: "Long live King Peter!" ("Ziveo Kralj Petar!")

Mishich moved from the window, to make place for a few younger officers, who were carrying the bloody and mutilated body of Queen Draga, with coarse jests and screaming as if they were mad.

They threw her into the garden.

Another group of officers had followed with the body of Alexander, covered with terrible wounds, yet still groaning in agony.

They raised him to throw him out of the window, but the fingers of the dying young man convulsively caught the frame of the window, and held it fast. One of the officers took his sword, and cut off his fingers. The next moment Alexander's body was thrown out, amidst the wild cries of his murderers —

"Ziveo Kralj Petar!"

Falling on the grass lawn of the garden, Alexander's body received such a shock that his right eye fell out of its socket! Still, he was not yet dead.

Two hours their bodies, naked, bleeding, and broken, were lying in the garden, in view of the soldiers! At four o'clock it began to rain. At that time the Russian Minister Tcharikoff crossed the narrow street from the Russian Legation, entered the flower garden, stopped, and, not without deep agitation, looked on the bodies of the man and woman who had been, only a few hours earlier, the King and Queen of Servia.

A few of the officers who had murdered them, with Colonel Mashin, stepped forward and saluted the Tzar's representative.

The first words of Tcharikoff were —

"For God's sake, gentlemen, carry their bodies inside the Palace. Do not leave them here in the rain, exposed to the gaze of the public."

A few moments after, two bed-sheets were brought out of the Palace. The murderers placed the bodies into these sheets and carried them into a room on the ground floor.

They noticed that one hand of King Alexander had grasped green grass from the lawn. In his death agony the convulsions of his fingers tore the soft grass.

Having murdered their King and Queen, and thrown them through the window into the front garden of the Palace, the murderers were seized by a sort of jubilant frenzy. They screamed and shouted at the top of their voices, dancing and running about the rooms like madmen, firing their revolvers at the pictures on the walls, at looking-glasses and candelabras; some of them broke with axes the bedstead of the Royal couple, and smashed all the fine things on the Queen's toilette table; called for wine from the King's cellars, and the trembling servants obeyed their orders. Others, who felt the air of the Palace hot and sulphurous, rushed into the courtyard, ordered tables to be set out on the carriage drive, and drank to the health of King Peter. For some time the Old Palace and its courtyard were turned into a pandemonium.

However shameful the orgie of these bloodthirsty officers, still more shameful was the behaviour of those murderers who kept cool.

I hope it is not true; but I have been assured by honourable men, and it was on different occasions stated in the papers, that many jewels belonging to the Queen, watches and rings belonging to the King, were taken away by these beasts in officers' uniform. Twelve hours before the King had received from the Treasury 100,000 francs (£4000), his monthly civil list, and, besides that amount, both the King and the Queen had always in reserve and at hand a sum of £4000. All that money disappeared during the mad tumult in the Palace immediately after the assassination of the Royal couple.

* * * * * * *

Meanwhile, during these bloody and horrible events in the Palace, several companies of soldiers marched in various directions. The officers who led them had special orders. A company surrounded the house of General Tzintzar-Markovich, who was with King Alexander up to nearly eleven o'clock that night, and was working in his room, fully dressed. At about one o'clock a.m. he was startled by a loud knock at the gate of his house. He opened the windows, and saw the soldiers.

"What do you want?" the General asked.

"General," said the commander of the company, Captain Svetozar Radakovich, "I have to give you a special communication by the order of his Majesty the King."

"Very well!" answered the General, and ordered his servant to open the door.

Entering the General's room, Captain Radakovich saluted and said —

"His Majesty ordered me to arrest you, and keep watch over you until further order!"

"Indeed!" said the General; and then added, "I will facilitate the accomplishment of your duty. Let us sit down. Take a cigarette."

They talked quietly, and apparently friendly, for some time. Then a servant from the General's daughter came running to ask Madame Tzintzar-Markovich to hurry to her daughter, who expected every moment to be confined. The poor young woman, hearing the detonations of dynamite and firing in the neighbourhood of the Palace, where her husband, the young and handsome Captain Miljkovich, was on duty as equerry, became terribly agitated, with the result that her confinement took place. At that moment her husband was lying dead in the Palace!

Captain Radakovich would not allow the General's wife to leave the house. But after both the General and Madame Tzintzar-Markovich implored him to let her go, promising faithfully not to tell anyone that the General was by the King's order under arrest, he gave her permission to go.

The General and Captain Radakovich continued talking and smoking for some time. Then the General proposed that they should have some coffee. He went towards the door to give orders that coffee should be made. Then Captain Radakovich also rose, took his revolver, and fired in quick succession several shots at the General, who fell instantly on his face, dead! His two unmarried daughters rushed into the room, and seeing their father dead, one of them lost her reason temporarily, and the other withdrew to a corner of the room, which she did not leave for several days and nights, remaining all the while speechless.

It was marvellous that Madame Tzintzar Markovich — herself a woman in very delicate health — was able to survive that awful night! She lost suddenly and most unexpectedly her husband and her son-in-law, saw her eldest daughter in danger of death by premature confinement, and both her younger daughters on the verge of insanity. Her husband was one of the ablest Servian officers, and a true Christian gentleman.

Colonel Mashin, who seemed to have acted as commander-in-chief of the conspiracy, had ordered Lieutenant Tankossich to murder the two young brothers of Queen Draga, Captains Nikodiyé and

Nicholas Lunyevitza. Captain Michael Yosipovich received orders to kill the War Minister, General Milovan Pavlovich, and the young Lieutenant Milosh R. Popovich to kill the Minister of Home Affairs (Police), Mr. Velya Todorovich.

Lieutenant Tankossich sent a detachment of soldiers to the house of the two brothers Lunyevitza. They were informed that they were wanted at once at the office of the staff of their division. At the office they were told by Colonel Solarovich that they were condemned to die. Lieutenant Tankossich brought them out in the yard, permitted them, at their own request, to embrace each other, and as good brothers to take leave of each other.

They were placed against the wall, facing bravely the firing party of soldiers. At a signal Tankossich made with his sword, the soldiers fired, and the two handsome and brave young men fell dead instantly, as most of the bullets struck them full in the face and forehead. By their conduct in bravely meeting death they did honour to their name.

It is positively asserted that their watches, rings, silver *tabatières*, and even their high patent boots were all taken from their dead bodies. I mention this, not only because such statements are persistently circulated, but because they are generally believed in Belgrade. It seems incredible that they can be true.

Another victim of the regicides was the Minister of War, General Milovan Pavlovich. He was an able officer, very strict commander, but, at the same time, one of the kindest men in the whole of Servia. Honest and loyal himself, he refused to believe that Servian officers could be so disloyal, and all the confidential reports about the conspiracy among the officers he treated as ridiculous inventions without the slightest foundation.

After the assassination of the King and the Queen, Colonel Mashin telephoned from the Palace to General Pavlovich's private residence, asking if the General was at home. The General's wife answered that he was, and, at the same time, wanted to know why they inquired after him. The answer came, not from Mashin, but from Lieutenant-Colonel Peter Mishich, "There are some disorders in the town, and we are sending a company of soldiers to protect the General!"

When the soldiers arrived before the house of the General, they, at the command of their captain, Michael Yosipovich, opened fire at once on the windows of the rooms on the first floor, in which the

General was known to live. He appeared, fully dressed, at one of the windows, and began to fire from a revolver on his assailants. Exposing himself at the window, he was soon wounded, but continued firing. Meanwhile a few soldiers, led by Lieutenant Milan Marinkovich, rushed up the staircase towards the door of the General's room. Marinkovich smashed the door with a dynamite cartridge, and by his own hand killed the General. Not satisfied with having murdered his chief, Marinkovich ordered a soldier to smash his skull with a blow from his rifle.

The General's widow, in describing the death of her husband, added that his murderers carried away his gold ring, and even a pair of new untried tall boots. In his purse they found altogether 80 francs (about £3. 3s.), of which they took 60, leaving the widow 20 francs. I suppose this money was taken by the common soldiers; but there are people who assert to have seen the ring of the General on the finger of his murderer, Marinkovich.

Colonel Mashin had selected the young Cavalry Lieutenant Milosh K. Popovich to kill the Home Minister, Velya Todorovich.

That officer entering the house of the Minister, and finding himself opposite a defenceless civilian, had not the courage to kill him. A few minutes later the murderer of General Pavlovich arrived and fired on the Minister, who fell at once. Believing him to be dead, the murderers left the house. Mr. Todorovich, who was only wounded, and had fainted, recovered consciousness, and took refuge with some neighbours.

Several other political and non-political men were on the list of those who were to be assassinated that early morning. Among others, Lieutenant George Petrovich, nephew of Queen Draga; and the editor of the *Male Novine*, Mr. Pera Todorovich, a devoted friend of King Alexander, and the most gifted of all the Servian journalists. The officer entrusted with the assassination of young Petrovich missed somehow his way, and returned to headquarters to ask for better directions to the house in which the Queen's nephew lived. Mr. Todorovich was informed an hour before the assassins came to his house, and he fled, and succeeded in crossing the river to Hungary. Meanwhile, that is between three and four o'clock in the morning, Colonel Mashin and the revolutionary Cabinet were informed by the Austro-Hungarian Minister that, if further assassinations did not stop, the Austrian army would occupy Belgrade. The murderous expeditions were at once stopped.

Having proclaimed Peter Karageorgevich King of Servia, from the window through which King Alexander's still palpitating body was thrown, Mishich and Mashin ordered the soldiers to decorate their caps with green branches and flowers from the Palace gardens, the military bands to march through the streets playing the gayest marches, and sent the gendarmes from house to house with orders to the proprietors to display the Servian national flags, in sign of the general rejoicing that the Obrenovich Dynasty was annihilated.

That was the tragic end of King Alexander and Queen Draga; but that was not the end of the tragedy of the Servian nation.

APPENDIX

THE PRINCIPAL CAUSES WHICH BROUGHT ABOUT THE TRAGIC END OF KING ALEXANDER AND QUEEN DRAGA.

WRITTEN BY A REGICIDE.

As I wished that *A Royal Tragedy* should be a fair statement of facts, a perfectly true and impartial history, I suggested to the chiefs of the regicides to let me have their own statement of causes and circumstances which led them to form the conspiracy for the assassination of King Alexander and Queen Draga. I offered them to publish their statement in the Appendix to my history of the great Tragedy.

They declined to do so, or rather, they refrained acting on my suggestion and offer.

But in the summer of 1905, when the desire of the Servian people to see Great Britain renewing diplomatic relations with Servia was intense, one of the regicides prepared something like a Memorandum of Justification of their action. It was specially prepared for the English Press, although it was written in French. It was sent to London, but until now it has nowhere been published. I leave out the introduction, which recapitulates the events of King Milan's reign, and also the last part, which simply pleads for the renewal of diplomatic relations between Great Britain and Servia, and I reproduce in what follows that part of the Memorandum which concerns King Alexander and the Conspiracy. I retain the title which the writer gave to his Memorandum: "*Principales causes qui amenerent la fin tragique du Roi Alexandre et de la Reine Draga.*" Those who know the real facts of the

Servian history during the last ten years will, on reading the following statement, necessarily come to the conclusion that the regicides' case must be exceedingly weak when they had need to falsify history and misrepresent the facts.

". . . Acting on the advice of his father, King Alexander gave, on the eve of the 1st of April 1892, a dinner in the Palace in honour of his Regents and their Ministers. At a certain moment he rose up and announced to his guests: That, from that time up to the dawn, they are his prisoners in the Palace; that the army is just then proclaiming him of full age and reigning King; and that from that moment he assumed full Royal powers! He added that he was acting thus because the Regents and their Ministers had violated the Constitution and disregarded the rights of the people. He published a proclamation to the people in which he said the same.

"This was King Alexander's first 'State's stroke' (*coup d'état*).

"A few weeks later he made, in the most solemn manner before the new Parliament, and into the hands of the Metropolitan of Servia, the oath of faithful respect for the Constitution and for the rights and liberties of the people.

"But already in the beginning of the autumn of that year he commenced to conspire, together with his mother Queen Nathalie, against the Radical regime, which he himself a few months ago had initiated. An underground struggle commenced between the King and the people, led by the Radicals. King Alexander tried to find political men who would support him in that struggle, made many experiments, and formed and dismissed numerous Cabinets. He brought into the political life of Servia still greater restlessness than that which prevailed under his father.

"In the commencement of the year 1897 he invited his father to return to Servia, disregarding entirely the law which forbade King Milan to come to or stay in the country. The judges refused to acknowledge the abolition of that law by the simple expression of the King's will. King Alexander answered by placing the judges on the retired list, and appointing new judges who approved of the irregular abolition of the Law against King Milan. This was King Alexander's second *coup d'état*.

"But finding it more and more difficult to reign according to his own will as long as the Constitution of 1888 was legally in vigour, Alexander, guided by the advice of his father Milan, tried to find opportunities to get rid of that, for him too Radical, Constitution. For that purpose he, through some officers of his household, arranged with a certain secret agent, Tchebinatz, a complot, the object of which was to provoke a revolution in the country. This fictitious complot gave him a pretext to put under arrest the most notable leaders of the Opposition, and to suspend the Constitution of 1888, replacing it by an old Constitution which to the representatives of the nation gave only the consultative vote. This was King Alexander's third *coup d'état*.

"All this was done only to enable King Alexander to renew the secret Treaty which his father concluded in 1882 with Austria; and also that his father, King Milan, might easier get money for the payment of his huge gambling debts. Just for that purpose he King Milan was appointed the Commander-in-Chief of the Servian Army.

"During all that time the entire Servian nation was in opposition to King Alexander's home and foreign policy. Europe did not know anything about it, because, as Austria had by the secret Treaty taken the engagement to protect the Obrenovich Dynasty, the entire Vienna Press diligently worked to conceal from Europe the state of things that prevailed in Servia, and the European Press generally went to Vienna for information on Servia.

"In order to destroy by a military tribunal the chiefs of the Radical Party, who never ceased their struggle for liberty, a new fictitious attempt against the life of King Milan was organised, and all the principal and the most courageous chiefs of the Opposition were arrested at the very moment when the attempt took place. A Royal decree proclaimed a Court-Martial, declaring that the judges of such a Court ought to give verdict according to their conscience and not according to the proofs. As members of that Court were appointed the most contemptible of men.

"The chiefs of the Opposition, arrested although quite innocent, were tortured by hunger, thirst, privation of sleep, and all sorts of torture. And finally they were condemned to prison, with hard labour, for life.

"To assure himself of the mastery over his son, King Milan allowed him to make intimate acquaintance with a widow, by name Draga Mashin, wife of a mining engineer who died by a mysterious death, and whose family believed that he was poisoned by her.

"Having a very small pension (not quite a hundred francs per month) she lived under the protection of certain men. She ceased to lead that disreputable life only when she succeeded in approaching the Court. And she came to the Court under the protection and special care of King Milan, who for several reasons wanted to see his son enter into liaison with such a woman.

"Somewhat later King Milan wanted to obtain for his son the hand of a German Princess, and the Servian Minister in Berlin received instructions to enter into negotiations with that object.

"But while King Milan was apparently with the consent and approval of his son working in that direction, King Alexander was thinking how to marry his mistress Draga Mashin. He succeeded in misleading his father and in cheating him. He sent his father to Carlsbad with a mission to arrange everything necessary for his marriage with the German Princess.

"Having got rid in that way of his father, he suddenly issued a proclamation announcing to the people that he had engaged himself with Draga, the granddaughter of 'Voyvode' Lunyevitza, and that he is going to marry her at once. As all his Ministers were opposed to that marriage he dismissed them, and, after many difficulties, formed a new Cabinet composed of most insignificant men.

"The Court officers and some of the Ministers made immediately a conspiracy to dethrone King Alexander and to reinstate King Milan. But political parties would not support that plan, fearing the wrath of the people if they brought King Milan back to the throne. And thus nothing came out of that Court conspiracy.

"The Radical Party, which had an immense majority in the country, but whose chiefs were either in prison or in exile, kept quiet. They saw that the end of the reigning dynasty was approaching, as the last Obrenovich, King Alexander, had taken for wife a woman of whom all Belgrade knew that she was unable to bear children.

"Possibly a revolution against King Alexander might have taken place at that juncture if the Emperor of Russia had not helped the marriage to take place by accepting to be the principal witness at the wedding!

"No one in Servia was satisfied with that marriage. Everybody felt that the dignity of Servia and of her King had been lowered. Everybody saw that the moment was approaching when the dynasty would collapse of itself. Love-letters of Draga Mashin to some of her former lovers were privately circulating in Belgrade, and could not but fill the readers with shame that Draga had become the Queen of Servia.

"King Alexander and Queen Draga did everything possible to approach the people and gain their love. They wanted to get from the people support against King Milan, whom they still feared, and who had wired to them that he would be the first to applaud the man who would drive them away from Servia. They hoped to get that support against the chiefs of all the parties, who suffered much by seeing the degradation of their fatherland. King Alexander gave amnesty to all political prisoners, recalled all political emigrants back to the country, and even offered to some of them to be Cabinet Ministers. On the whole, King Alexander and Queen Draga had no success in that endeavour, except that they won some politicians of low standing.

"A few months after the marriage it was officially announced to the people that the Queen was in an interesting condition! Then commenced that comedy, unique in the history of the world by its cynicism. All that was necessary to keep the people in illusion was done with the greatest care. The people were divided in two groups: one which judging only by appearances believed that the Queen was really in an interesting condition; and the other, composed of men who knew Draga, and who believed that she was simulating intentionally, and deliberately cheating everybody.

"The Emperor of Russia, who was by proxy the principal witness at King Alexander's wedding, and who had promised to receive at his Court Alexander and Draga, got such proofs of Draga's simulation that he insisted King Alexander should consent that a specialist whom he (the Emperor) wished to send should examine the real condition of the Queen.

"The King was obliged to receive the Russian specialist. He no doubt hoped that he would be able, in one way or other, to obtain from him the confirmation of the Queen's statement that she was with child. But he was mistaken. The Imperial accoucheur found that the Queen was not enceinte! But he was so far obliging towards the Queen that he added that a sort of tumour had been formed which could quite naturally mislead anyone.

"This brought a new consternation to the people, a new humiliation and shame! Everybody now saw clearly what was the intention of the Royal couple, namely, to cheat the people and to declare somebody else's baby as Queen Draga's child.

"To quiet the people, and to give them some sort of consolation, King Alexander re-established the Constitution of 1888 (which he had suspended in 1897), but with some important additions; as, for instance, the creation of a Second Chamber (the Senate). He hoped thereby to win the richer and higher class of the people, who as

Senators would probably act as a brake against the Radical Party. He gave that Constitution without consulting the people, in fact again by a *coup d'état*. Anyhow, he made a solemn oath, in the presence of both Chambers and of Queen Draga, to respect faithfully the new Constitution.

"Having not succeeded with the plan of substituting somebody's baby for their own, and so cheating the people in that way, and as the doctors declared that Queen Draga never could have children, the King and the Queen gave up that first plan definitely, and decided to do something else, not less dangerous; namely, to proclaim one of the Queen's brothers as Heir-Apparent of the throne! Their choice fell on the younger of the two brothers, on Nikodiyé Lunyevitza.

"To prepare the ground and accustom the people to this idea, the King began to raise the position of the Queen's brothers and to treat them as if they were Princes of Royal blood. He organised quite an agitation in the army in favour of Nikodiyé. The younger brother was chosen by the King and Queen instead of the elder one, simply because he was somewhat less bad than his brother.

"The two brothers Lunyevitza, themselves young officers, began to gather around them other young officers, and by presents and other courtesies and kindnesses to gain them for the intentions of the Royal couple. Officers who refused such advances, and would not have anything to do with the two Lieutenants Lunyevitza, were persecuted and insulted. King Alexander gave the order that whenever the brothers Lunyevitza, or one of them, entered a barrack or a camp, the guards were to be called out to present arms, and the Commander was to give them the usual military reports. This caused at once a great dissatisfaction in the army against those two 'officer-princes' who were so arbitrarily imposed on it. Hardly ever a day passed that they had not some words, quarrels, and conflicts with officers. Often it came to scandalous scenes between the officers and themselves on account of the privileged position which they assumed.

"King Alexander went a step further. He requested the Government to submit to the Parliament a Bill enacting the inviolability of the two brothers of the Queen. The Cabinet, although generally quite humble servants of the King and Queen, dared not propose such a Bill. The King then began to agitate personally among the Senators, who by majority were Radicals, to promise to support his demands. They refused to give such a promise. He requested them then to resign their mandates as Senators, that they might be replaced by others who would be more pliable to his will, and he promised them all sorts of personal advantages. They persisted in their refusal. Thereupon the King began to denounce the Senate as an institution which pushes itself like a wedge between the King and the people, and publicly expressed his conviction that the Senate ought to be abolished, or at least that in some way its members ought to be replaced by others.

"Seeing that the army refused to treat the Queen's brothers as Princes of Royal blood, seeing that the Senators would never consent that one of the Lieutenants Lunyevitza should be proclaimed Heir-Apparent to the throne of Servia, King Alexander decided for another *coup d'état*. He formed a new Cabinet, which was prepared to help him to do it. Many honest State's employés, especially among the prefects and police commissioners, were either dismissed or transferred to some other place and service. They were replaced generally by men of bad reputation, known as unscrupulous and even as dishonest. When the King's attention was drawn to this fact, he answered: 'It is of such men that I have need; honest and scrupulous men are not willing to help me to get a Parliament which would be ready to accept my proposals!'

"The excitement and exasperation of the people were great, and growing from day to day. The patriots began to talk loudly that it was high time to save Servia, and especially that the Queen ought to be sent away or, if necessary, strangled and murdered, the woman who imposed herself on the nation being not personally worthy to enter the humblest house of an honourable citizen, and who now wanted to impose on the country one of her brothers as heir to the throne. The dissatisfaction spread to all classes, and carried away with it young and old. The officers composing the household of the King and the Queen expressed to their comrades in the army that they regret to have to serve such a King and such a Queen. Even the numerous detectives, who were chosen to spy everything and everybody in the service of Alexander and Draga, were making common cause with the malcontents, and communicated to them the orders which they received from the Minister of Police or from the Court.

"A small demonstration without importance, organised by the University students and commercial assistants and clerks, developed into a serious riot. All the town passed on the side of the demonstrants, and the soldiers called out to disperse them sympathised, and in some places fraternised, with them. The officers who received from the

Palace order by telephone to fire on the people, refused to do so without written orders according to the prescription of the law. The people felt and saw that the army was with them, and that gave them courage, and they were prepared to do anything. The King and the Queen became terrified, and thought that the critical moment had arrived.

"The King ordered several regiments to come to the capital, and in the night of the 25th March (1903) he executed again a *coup d'état*. He suspended the Constitution which he gave in 1901. The suspension lasted only half an hour, time enough for him to sign decrees by which all the members of the Senate, the State Council, and the Court of Accounts who were, according to the old Constitution, nominated for life were dismissed from their positions and replaced by others.

"After this his Cabinet (General Tzintzar-Markovich) undertook new general elections, using, according to the instructions from the King, all sorts of illegal pressure on the electors, and by such means it succeeded in securing a sufficiently large majority of the deputies.

"But to succeed entirely in their heart's desire the King and the Queen made a diabolical scheme. It was arranged that it should be proven by false documents and false witnesses that certain officers and certain politicians had made a complot to murder the King and Queen while they were walking or driving in the Deer-Park near Belgrade. A man was hired who would apparently fire at them (but without hurting them), who would be immediately arrested, and who would then name before the Court those officers and politicians as men who had hired him to murder the Royal couple. This fictitious attempt was to take place on the eve of the meeting of the new Parliament, to which then would immediately be submitted, as the matter of absolute urgency, the Bill appointing Nikodiyé Lunyevitza as Heir-Apparent to the throne.

"The friends of King Milan, who on the eve of Alexander's marriage with Draga wished to recall Milan to the throne, now, since Milan had died in exile, joined the officers of the army, who were determined not to allow that their future King should be a Lunyevitza whom they despised. They were joined also by the officers of the Court, who were disgusted in witnessing what was done in the Palace, and what the King and Queen were preparing to do.

"Destiny had willed that at the Court of the last Obrenovich, served as an equerry the grandson of that Naoumovich who was killed defending Kara-George against the murderers sent by Prince Milosh

(Obrenovich the First). Everything that was necessary to penetrate into the Palace was arranged with that officer. He perished, together with those whom he delivered to the conspirators.

"The officers who were ready to sacrifice their lives in order to save the country from new massacres (?) and from unworthy heirs to the throne, had the intention to accomplish their object on Palm Sunday, in the fortress where, according to custom, the King was to come; but he did not come. Then they were prepared to do it on the occasion of the foundation stone for the Palace of Music being laid down by the King and Queen; but again they did not appear. Then they thought to kill the King and Queen in the circus, to which they went frequently; but they gave up that plan on account of the many children and other people who might innocently suffer. But having been informed of the King's arrangement for a false attempt and its consequences, and seeing that they had not much time to lose, they in the night of the 29th May (11th June N.S.) penetrated into the Palace and accomplished their object.

"If the drama was accomplished under conditions which are very regrettable and perhaps shameful, that happened against the intention of the actors. It came about in consequence of the officers believing themselves betrayed and trapped, and also because after two or three hours of searching for Alexander and Draga in the Palace, it was absolutely necessary to prove to the soldiers and to the people that the King and the Queen were really dead. When they entered the Palace the conspirators did not intend to do the victims to such a horrible death, but when the sword is once drawn and when the fight begins no one can foresee how it will end.

"It is natural to regret such an end, but at the same time it is right to recognise that after all a good people had suffered from their King, and after the manner in which that King had treated his own father and mother some such terrible end was to be expected."

In this statement of a Regicide there is much that is true, but at least as much that is not true.

It is quite true that King Alexander was not a constitutional monarch. By his bad education, by his surroundings, by political circumstances of Servia, by the follies of the leaders of political parties in Servia, he had been encouraged in his autocratic proclivities. I am the last man who would undertake to justify his numerous "State strokes" (*coups d'état*), but it is only fair to remember that Alexander, like his father Milan, was obliged day and night to defend himself against the permanent conspiracy which was working by all and every means to replace the dynasty Obrenovich on the throne of Servia by the dynasty Karageorgevich.

It is quite true that King Alexander behaved — since his marriage with Draga — cruelly towards his father and mother. I myself told him once that he will have to suffer for his conduct towards his parents, and implored him to change his conduct towards them.

It is quite true that he ought not to have made Draga Mashin the Queen of Servia, and it is quite true that the army and the Servian political world disapproved of that marriage.

But it is not true that Draga Mashin led a dissolute life before she came into contact with the Court. It is not true that King Milan brought her in the way of his son.

It is not true that Queen Draga simulated, with the approval of King Alexander, as if she had been in an interesting condition, desiring to proclaim some other woman's baby as her own. She *in good faith* thought herself to be *enceinte*, and not only all the Court and friends of the dynasty who saw her believed so, but competent doctors and specialists — not only the Servian physicians to the Court, but specialists of European fame, brought from Paris and Vienna — did believe so. The well-known French accoucheur, Dr. Collet, gave to the King a written assurance that the Queen was in an interesting condition. Nor is it true that the Tzar insisted that two Russian specialists, whom he wished to send, must examine the real condition of the Queen. Dr. Sneguireff and Dr. Goobareff were invited by King Alexander and Queen Draga to attend her at her expected confinement, and acting on their first impressions they, on their arrival in the Belgrade Palace, ordered all necessary preparations for an accouchement. The story of her alleged plot to cheat everybody shows only how boundless was the hatred of some of her personal enemies, and how the agents working for the downfall of the dynasty Obrenovich did not hesitate to use the most abominable lies only to discredit that dynasty.

It is quite true that the reports were assiduously spread that King Alexander, hypnotised by Queen Draga, wished to proclaim Nikodiyé Lunyevitza, her younger brother, Heir-Apparent to the throne. It is true that such reports alarmed the people and disgusted many officers, especially younger ones, the comrades of Nikodiyé. But all those reports were repeatedly and emphatically contradicted officially, and denied by King Alexander on several solemn occasions to the members of Parliament, to the deputations from the people, to foreign diplomatists, etc. Eight days before his assassination he confided to the uncle of his father, Aleko Catargi (at present the Roumanian Minister in London), that his intention was to adopt a young boy of a small German Court, to bring him and educate him in Servia and make him heir to the Servian Crown.

It is certainly not true that the attempt on King Milan's life was only a fictitious attempt arranged by Milan himself and his son Alexander in order to get rid of certain Radical political leaders.

And I honestly believe that the story about the plot which the regicides say was projected by King Alexander against himself, in order to make numerous arrests of oppositionists and frighten the Parliament into submission and readiness to proclaim Nikodiyé Heir-Apparent, is simply an invention of the regicides themselves to justify their action. After the assassination of King Alexander and Queen Draga they got into their hands the King's private papers and secret Archives of the Court and of the State, and they never produced the slightest document proving that King Alexander really was arranging, or had arranged, such a diabolical plot.

There is no doubt that several unconstitutional acts of King Alexander, his marriage with Draga Mashin, and then more especially the phantom of Nikodiyé Lunyevitza as future King of Servia, created intense dissatisfaction among the officers — especially the younger ones — of the army. That dissatisfaction was cleverly used by the leaders of the anti-dynastic movement, and it succeeded in annihilating the dynasty Obrenovich in a horrible manner, which added a new bloody page to the history of the Servian nation, certainly to the great and everlasting regret of all Servian patriots.

Other reprints available in this series

Life of Alexander II, F.E. Grahame
Alexander III, Tsar of Russia, Charles Lowe
The Intimate Life of the Last Tsarina, Princess Catherine Radziwill
My mission to Russia and other diplomatic memories, Sir George Buchanan
The reign of Rasputin: An empire's collapse, M.V. Rodzianko
Collected Works: Once a Grand Duke, Always a Grand Duke, Twilight of Royalty, Alexander, Grand Duke of Russia

Frederick, Crown Prince and Emperor, Rennell Rodd
Letters of the Empress Frederick, edited by Sir Frederick Ponsonby
Between two Emperors: The Willy-Nicky Telegrams and Letters, 1894-1914
Potsdam Princes, Ethel Howard

My Past, Marie Larisch
The Story of my Life (Vols. I-III in one volume), Marie, Queen of Roumania

Richard III, Sir Clements Markham

The Complete Works: The Journal of a Disappointed Man, A Last Diary, Enjoying Life and other Literary Remains, W.N.P. Barbellion

For further details please see *amazon.co.uk/amazon.com*

Manufactured by Amazon.ca
Bolton, ON